Black Dog Publishing

NEW DIRECTIONS IN JEWELLERY

INTRODUCTION

Catherine Grant

This book looks at the increasingly varied ways in which the boundaries of traditional jewellery design are being extended and challenged. Encompassing work that crosses the disciplines of fine art, performance, sculpture, textiles and fashion design, New Directions in Jewellery showcases makers currently working within this broadening discipline — from those who are manipulating the properties of metal to conceptual works that critique the cultural and social meanings that have built up around the wearing and manufacture of jewellery.

The three essays here propose a number of ways of looking at jewellery design, beginning with the question that Paul Derrez poses: "What kind of jewellery are we actually talking about?" Derrez, a well-known maker and owner of the influential Galerie Ra in The Netherlands, presents an account of conceptual approaches to jewellery that he sees coming from the work of avant-garde makers in the 1960s. Proposing ways of re-invigorating jewellery design today, Derrez calls for an expansion of the influences to be incorporated in current practice, suggesting that street style and customisation offer routes to think about jewellery outside of its traditional definitions. Jivan Astfalck, a jeweller and writer concerned with the processes and narratives around jewellery, discusses work under the heading "Jewellery Art". These works cross over with installation and fine art, such as Ted Noten's Chewing Gum brooches, which use usually discarded material as the basis for precious and beautiful adornment, as well as a process-based 'fine art' activity. In the last essay, Caroline Broadhead draws out the dialogue between jewellery practice and fine art by considering the interaction and implication for jewellery on the wearer's and the viewer's bodies. Broadhead, whose own conceptual practice crossed over from jewellery to textile and installation work, sees jewellery as activating a space of interaction between wearer and viewer, considering the eroticised and intimate site of the mouth as one example of the places in which jewellery can be used in unexpected and emotionally charged ways.

Following the essays, a wide range of jewellers — from eminent figures like Gerda Flöckinger through to makers who have emerged in the last few years —

are divided into loose thematic sections. Most of the jewellers featured here could easily be placed in more than one of these sections, so the intention is not to construct a framework that fixes the work, but instead to provide ways into a vast array of approaches, styles and attitudes. The opening section, "Organic Forms", is indicative of this organising principle. Considering works that look to nature for inspiration, this section includes the formal employment of motifs derived from flowers and plants, the apparently abstract pieces by Dorothy Hogg that are based on the interior networks of the body, and the installation work of Hilde de Decker, who literally grows her jewellery by combining it with vegetables, distorting the shapes of tomatoes and peppers as they grow through and around the metal.

The next section, "Small Statements", concentrates on the conceptual use of jewellery. Often focussing on the symbolic function of jewellery and creating works that are more sculptural than wearable, the jewellers included here span the work of Mah Rana, with her encased wedding rings, His 'n Hers, 1995/2002, to fantasies of biotechnology, in which jewellery is grown on the surface of the body, as in the work of Norman Cherry. "Fashion Forward" moves the emphasis from the idea to the look, with a group of jewellers who are engaged with the world of fashion — from the catwalk to celebrity bling. Elisabeth Galton's large sculptural pieces echo the high fashion outfit that is about fantasy and provocation rather than practicality, whilst Daisuke Sakaguchi's graffiti inspired work takes street style and reworks it in heavy silver, supplying his creations to fashion and celebrity clients.

"Tactile Sculpture" moves from fashion to textiles, with the work in this section drawing on the techniques of fabric production, as well as considering the impact of large sculptural objects on the movement of the body. In the seminal pieces by Arline Fisch, metal is worked as if it was yarn to create large scale collars and cuffs. Many of the younger makers in this section can be seen to be expanding on her practice, with the incorporation of textile techniques to create oversized objects that almost cross over from jewellery to costume or sculpture.

Other makers included in this section challenge the properties of the material they use, contouring latex to the body, constricting and highlighting aspects of the wearer's body so that the jewellery is only completed when worn. In opposition to this approach, the following section "New Geometries" focuses on works that, rather than looking to the body for a starting point, turn instead to the basic geometric forms — circles, squares, triangles. Drawing on the formalist works from the previous decades by jewellers such as David Watkins, the jewellers in this section find different ways to invigorate these abstract forms, often made in productive tension with the contours of the body that the pieces are to be worn on.

"Telling Stories" returns to the conceptual based practice as seen in "Small Statements", with the makers in this section concerned with narrative and memory, utilising a huge range of techniques and aesthetics. From the Dada inspired assemblages of Hans Stofer to the unwritten pages in the miniature books of Alyssa dee Krauss, the makers each approach an idea of history and story telling and find ways to communicate through jewellery, starting with anything from conventional gold and silver to found objects.

The last two sections consider formal qualities of jewellery, with the first, "Colour and Light", featuring makers who utilise the colours and transparencies of resins, plastics and glass. From the glowing pieces of Nicolas Estrada to the neon colours of Anoush Waddington, the jewellers in this section have pushed the ways in which materials are used in their work to create vibrant and arresting colour palettes. The last section in the book, "Decorative Elements", celebrates the qualities of adornment and decoration that are embedded in the history of jewellery, valorising the opulent, the baroque and the beautiful. Peter Chang's highly patterned and technically advanced use of acrylic appears to have almost been grown rather than made, whilst the work of Gerda Flöckinger utilises precious stones and metals in ornate and intricate constellations that have put her at the forefront of experimental jewellery design for the last five decades. These well-known jewellers are shown alongside newer practitioners such as Anna Lewis, who manipulates the natural beauty of feathers in her delicate and ephemeral works.

Altogether, New Directions in Jewellery is not a manifesto of what jewellery should be, but rather a presentation of the numerous ways in which it is developing, both in dialogue with its own history, as well as with other visual disciplines. Returning to Derrez's question, "What kind of jewellery are we actually talking about?", this book seeks to offer the answer in a multitude of directions, styles and concepts. By grouping the work presented in this book, the different narratives that run through the jewellery can be shown as fluid and cross-pollinating. Rather than presenting a trend or a movement, the wide variety of jewellery in these pages show how there are themes and motivations that tie together different work, whilst not pinning down a fundamental set of terms or ideas. From small scale brooches to body sized sculptural objects, issues that cross over the entire book are the ways in which considerations of material intersect with conceptual theses, with the telling of stories alongside the tactile possibilities of the body and adornment. The jewellers featured in New Directions in Jewellery are engaged with definitions of jewellery, in terms of its cultural identity, the way it affects its wearer and the history and significance of the materials used to make the pieces shown. To find out what kind of jewellery we are talking about here, read on.

JEWELLERY?
WHAT KIND OF JEWELLERY ARE
WE ACTUALLY TALKING ABOUT?

Paul Derrez

For the wider public there are standard mass-produced pieces — shiny, glittering, easy-to-wear necklaces, rings, bracelets and earrings. Easy in the sense of readily being recognised as jewellery — they do not evoke questions or debate — and at the same time easy in a practical sense due to their limited size, flexibility and standard fastenings. They can be expensive or inexpensive, precious or semi-precious, durable or semi-durable. Sold through jewellers and department stores, this kind of jewellery is found at its most stereotypical in the international airport shopping mall. Alongside these staid mass-market examples, there is the constantly evolving fashion market for accessories — a market aimed at change, in fact. Ambience, colour, form and material are all adapted to the constantly changing fashion image, offered in department stores and clothes shops through trendy displays. There is also jewellery marketed to a wide audience from non-western societies; sometimes unique, old, expensive and based on local traditions, but more often mass-produced, cheap and made for the tourist. Fashion stylists ransack this ethnic market for its potential usefulness for fashion trends, and then have what they find tailored to market demands and produced in bulk elsewhere.

Alongside high street designs, exclusive labels offer jewellery, which is hardly exclusive in design and edition, but more in 'image' and price. Costly advertising campaigns create the necessary brand image. Prestige is the keyword here and they scream out to be copied. A marketing initiative of original designs can be seen, among others, at the German firm of Niessing. The company executes designs from designers working within or outside the company. They bring a collection with a refined, pared-down language of form — slick, clean, pure craftsmanship. Carl Dau, also in Germany, produces jewellery with an industrial cool edge. These companies are more an innovative workspace than a factory, guaranteeing a certain degree of exclusivity through distribution via a restricted dealer network.

1   Maria Hees, Garden Hose Bracelet, 1978, plastic

2   Gijs Bakker, Ferrari Dino 206 SD, brooch, 2001, fire opal, silver, photo and acrylic

3

Svenja John, brooches, 2004, polycarbonate

Then there are the smaller, alternative markets, like the silversmiths who sell more specialised items, sometimes made themselves, but often purchased from larger distributors. Here, the unique and personal aspect is well promoted but in reality the choice is often from versions of existing designs, materials and techniques. Trade fairs like those in Frankfurt and Munich supply all the ingredients, which when put together in new combinations, appear to be artistically innovative, but in fact are usually tasteful or tasteless 'frippery'.

Finally, there is the category of 'art jewellery', although 'author' jewellery would be a better name as it is made by one 'author' who decides the concept and design. This is a category that has largely been realised and become more professionalised over the last 30 years. This approach is a result of the progression through the recent history of jewellery and art, so before considering contemporary works, let us cast a backward glance.

  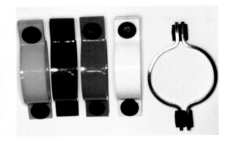

Gijs Bakker, Stovepipe Necklace and Bracelet, 1967, anodised aluminium

Pierre Degen, Screen with partly wearable objects, 1981, mixed media

Hans Appenzeller, Serie Sieraad Bracelets, 1973, acrylic and rubber

When in the late 1960s traditional social, political and cultural structures began to be broken down, there was simultaneously an invigorating and exciting experimentation in jewellery design. This experimentation continued throughout the 1970s and 80s, as complete freedom was created regarding form, material, technique, production methods, serial production and jewellery's relationship to the body — anything became possible. In Britain, The Netherlands, Germany, Switzerland and Austria, especially, there was much innovation and experimentation. Jewellery could be a statement, a mass-produced product, an accessory, a DIY kit, a clothing addition, a photographic prop, wearable sculpture, a costume or stage pieces. Collaborating with colleagues and other disciplines was challenging and also necessary in order to achieve disparate and thought provoking results. These were 'golden' years in which creativity and personal development were considered more important than marketability. However, this 'safe haven' situation was not to be blessed with a long life. The serial production of jewellery, which in reality was traditional assemblage, declined due to the weak link between

production, distribution and marketing. Several designers of serially produced jewellery began to focus on other industrial products. Alongside this decline, the opening presented by fashion also appeared to have no future. In fashion speed and teamwork is the essence and the traditionally and individually trained jewellery designers were not equipped for this. Later, political and social changes (specifically Thatcherism) propelled a hard, realistic approach in the form of efficiency and financial results.

What was achievable at this time was the direction of jewellery as an art form. What developed were forms of jewellery that did not comply with a demand (which by definition is always based on the recognition factor). A new demand or need was defined. As in science, this process evolved via research and experimentation towards a wide range of conclusions and results, with specialised departments in polytechnics and universities leading the way. These departments, usually originating from applied arts courses, mainly functioned in an isolated manner, without interaction with design or fashion. Similar to the art sector, in recent decades a worldwide and specialist infrastructure for jewellery has been created with its own training programmes and galleries, museum collections and collectors, books and catalogues. Priority lies with developing new meaning and a new language of form — a new aesthetic. Any kind of material and technique can be used, but often research takes place within a small field and within strict boundaries. Due to the individual studio aspect of production, advanced technology is rarely used, as the availability and financial feasibility of using cutting edge technology is impossible on this scale. Only a few training programmes succeed in linking up innovative technology with innovative ideas, such as the Royal College of Art in London. It is enviable that such an interaction exists between design, marketing and technology in other accessory

Lam de Wolf, collar, 1983, textile

Otto Künzli, Wallpaper Brooch, 1983, foam and wallpaper

Marjorie Schick, Body-Piece, 1986, wood

Maria Blaisse, Spheres,
1989, industrial foam

Frank Tjepkema,
Bling Bling, pendant, 2003,
gold-plated metal

fields, like shoes, spectacles and mobile phones. Due to the lack of
technological innovation within jewellery design, the danger exists that all
meaningful innovation remains elitist and socially irrelevant, although this
is changing slowly.

There are jewellery designers and promoters who would like to see more
innovative approaches to jewellery, and are trying to develop them. Gijs Bakker
and Marijke Vallanzesca started up their Chi ha paura...? label in 1996, with an
ever expanding collection of jewellery by artists and designers, professionally
produced and distributed. However, pre-existing designs which have been chosen
for the collection appear to have more success than the ones initiated by the
label, illustrating how difficult it is to introduce new ideas successfully. In a
museum-shop-ambiance this Chi ha paura...? formula seems to work. Another
example is the Austrian jewellery designer Florian Ladstätter, who is also very
interested in reaching a new, young clientele. Some of his pieces refer to tools
and electronic gadgets, others point to sexuality or become clothing accessories.
He aims to reach a larger audience through the actual nature of his designs,
and modes of presentation that are in keeping with fashion and stunning live
shows. For Ladstätter, showing pieces in a gallery situation does not access a
broad enough audience.

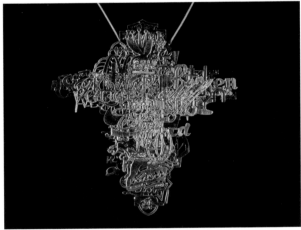

A successful breakthrough on a large scale seems only possible by infiltrating
the fashion world itself. Only there do teams of specialists ensure a coherent
whole between innovation, production, distribution and marketing. For an
individual designer this is still as yet unachievable. We are waiting for the

moment that jewellers are invited to develop collections of innovative jewellery for fashion labels like Nike. The attempt by Swatch could be seen to be moving in this direction but the results are more styling than innovation. A country that might be able to develop jewellery design in this direction is Japan. The multitude of wealthy design- and fashion- conscious kids and young adults provide a large potential market for Japanese high quality producers. The Hiko Mizuno Jewellery College in Tokyo, with its variety of specialisms and young teaching staff, which has expanded enormously in the last ten years, is a perfect base for such a development.

Florian Ladstätter,
pendant, 2001, plastics

Noam Ben-Jacov, Room,
1987, aluminium, nylon
and steel,
175 x 280 x 250 cm,
photography:
Noam Ben-Jacov,
dancer: Ziv Frenkel

There are also the creative consumers who can affect trends themselves. For example, a trend such as the wearing of a heavy chain on which keys or a purse are 'secured' via a belt and trouser pocket must have originated somewhere. These street-styles are interesting since they have an immense impact on mainstream fashion and design, and the trends occur in a continually changing dialogue with urban culture. From this perspective, it would be a positive step for jewellery artists to adopt a more playful approach to their research, and perhaps look to incorporate urban styling and street phenomena into their work. A start in this direction has already been taken. The German-based group Chicks on Speed are engaged in music and performance but also clothing and jewellery, using a punk, DIY aesthetic. They make costumes out of paper and found materials, giving instructions on how to construct similar outfits, undermining the commercial fashion system. Could the stage also then be a platform for new developments in jewellery on a larger scale?

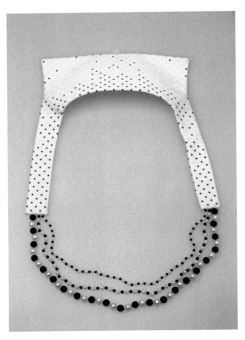

Manon van Kouswijk (The Netherlands) uses a combination of materials and techniques, such as embroidery, because of their 'emotional' qualities. In her work, seemingly unimportant memories are shown to be nevertheless much-loved and cherished.

Necklace, 2004, textiles, pearls and onyx beads

Susanne Klemm (The Netherlands) uses an unambiguous language in her clear and humorous jewellery designs. Speaking with imagery taken from today's visual assault, she isolates and abstracts forms.

Fire and Fired, rings, 2002, silver and lacquer

Bettina Speckner (Germany) goes further back in time and combines techniques from the early years of photography with nostalgic images — sometimes manipulated in such a way that a narrative alienation occurs.

Brooch, 2002, ferrotype, silver and jade

Warwick Freeman (New Zealand) lets the qualities of his country speak when using specific materials like shell or volcanic rock as well as the symbolic and the sign languages of the Pacific.

Sentence, brooches, 2003, mixed media

| 5 | 6 |
| 7 | 8 |

Daniel Kruger (Germany) is an accomplished worker in precious metals. He is inspired by non-Western cultures and historic example, yet his personal and contemporary approach make his jewellery designs unique and of the present.

Necklace, 2004, silver, gold, cornelian and silk

Nel Linssen (The Netherlands) has been making jewellery from paper for about 15 years. She glues it into layers and punches out the mainly circular forms. These elements are then folded and combined into necklaces and bracelets. By endlessly experimenting, she has developed an impressive refinement in her work in terms of movement, structure and colour.

Necklace, 2001, paper

Karl Fritsch (Germany) makes an ironic statement about classical jewellery through exaggeration. His designs are striking statements for powerful personalities.

Rings, 2004, gold, silver, rubies, sapphire, diamonds and emeralds

Johanna Dahm (Switzerland) learnt a special casting technique with the Ashanti in Ghana and employs this technique for a new, personal language of form.

Rings, 2000, gold

Jewellery as a Fine Art Practice

Jivan Astfalck

Jewellery is a multi-faceted and vibrant art form, which exists at quite different levels of commerce, design and fine art. An object created as a commodity to succeed in a post-capitalistic market needs to be examined and understood in a different way than an object which has a conceptual, narrative or purely formal agenda as its driving force. Not only for the sake of art historical and critical clarity, but also for the makers themselves and an appreciating public, it has become increasingly important to differentiate between the contrasting, and sometimes conflicting, attitudes and approaches which are brought to the making of jewellery and to acknowledge the distinct contributions these jewellery practices make to visual culture.

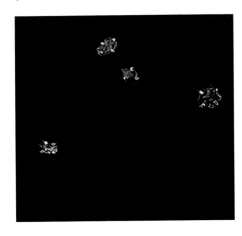 

Kadri Mälk, Cassiopeia, brooch, 2004, silver, gold and garnet

Kadri Mälk, Andromeda, brooch, 2004, silver, gold and aquamarine

photography:
Tiit Rammul

Jewellery brings to the fine art discussion a distinct sensibility of the relationship between object and the body in its wider sense. It might be helpful in this context to consider a distinction between three critical positions regarding the status of the jewellery object. The first position treats the object as an independent entity maybe a piece of jewellery or clothing. Even though these objects have been generated by design processes, have definable sculptural identity and can be formally analysed, they offer nothing in excess of decoration when worn on the body. The second position, by contrast, is occupied by a generation of artists whose conceptual concerns transgress the definable object; the object literally merges with the body. Conceptual work such as this makes visible the fuzzy boundary between the body-related but independent object and what is more appropriately termed Body Art. The third position considers the object in dialogue with its framing device, this might be the body itself, social or psychological phenomena or other theoretical concerns. In excess of their own materiality and formal qualities, objects made in this mode have often strong narratives inscribed, which are concerned with the symbolic and emotional investment we all have in the objects we make, wear and love. Such objects can be used as devices for the visible transmission of messages, a way of communicating by means of visual signs and signals.

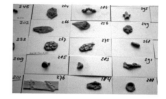

Jewellery as a fine art practice could not exist without its historical and traditional roots in materials and processes, adornment and ornamentation. A generation of jewellery artists are practicing now who have not only been trained within the tight parameters of a skills-oriented craft, but have also been educated by studio crafts people, who themselves revolutionised jewellery design in the 1960s and 70s. Then, ideas of bourgeois taste and status were challenged by jewellers with a passion for modernist form, sculptural identity and a much wider interest in different materials. Now, informed by current visual culture and the history and theory of modern art, new artistic strategies and enquiries are being formulated.

It is not necessarily the 'art-full' crafting of the object or an obvious radical aesthetic which defines some jewellery as a fine art practice; but, more interestingly, it is the integrity of enquiry, knowledge of contemporary cultural issues, confidence in using artistic strategies and the thought processes which inform the making practice and thus push the boundaries of the discipline. These artistic methodologies differ from a 'classical' design process in so far as they take their dynamic from a content-based enquiry rather than from a purely formal, material-based or skill-driven approach. The aesthetics of different jewellery artists' work are frequently developed by this process of enquiry, rather than being the stated aim of their practice. In the case of Ted Noten's Chewing Gum, 1999, the fact that most frequently used pavements in most European cities are littered with bubble-gum stains led to the idea to ask people to "chew their own brooch". The project was set up in the Museum Booijmans van Beuningen, Rotterdam and 800 people followed the invitation to chew their own brooch.

1

Ted Noten, Chewing Gum, 1999, chewing gum brooches cast in bronze, silver and gold

Ruudt Peters, images
taken from Peters' book
Change, 2002, showing a
piece of his jewellery,
Lapis-Xanthosis, 1996,
8.5 x 6.5 x 8.5 cm,
alongside a photograph by
Rob Veksluys, Amsterdam

The winning entry of a juried competition was then cast in 24 ct gold and finalised as a wearable piece of jewellery. What was at first recognised as an 'ornamentation' of debatable aesthetic value littering our environment, was re-configured and re-introduced as a precious piece of body adornment, thus re-arranging the everyday order of things.

The thought processes which inform most of Jewellery Art unfold across larger groups of work, rather than an individual piece, and are often dependent on careful staging and environments. This trend required jewellery artists to look for new presentation formats and different exhibition opportunities. Photography, video, installation and performance, interactive work generated in social contexts and artist collaborations have become environments in which such work can be situated. This does not, in my view, mean that the work has lost its identity as jewellery. Jewellery Art is informed by these other art disciplines, but does not so much address them within their own self-referential histories; rather these other disciplines are used as framing devices for the all-important work, the jewellery object.

Objects framed and presented in installation or photographic/video contexts enable new possibilities of visual perception and subsequently interpretation and understanding. The often rather more 'introverted' objects acquire heightened theatricality and performativity; a powerful strategy giving more artistic control over the interpretative reading of the work. Hidden layers of meaning can be

played with, as the objects assume new identities while dialogically interacting with their environment. What is denied is a standard version of what is commonly thought of as jewellery; what is created is the condition for the emergence of new dimensions of experience and reality, and the possibility that old and empty worlds, old and tired formulae, can be made new.

In the case of my own work this dynamic is explored by placing replica of traditional pieces of jewellery onto early 1960s 'Steiff' animals. The jewellery has been made specifically to suit the characters of the soft toy animals, which have been collected over two years. These animals have been chosen because they are exquisitely made, have 'collectors value' in their own right and refer to the autobiographical aspects of the work. Their cute pre-Disney nostalgic quality replaces the traditional display prop and re-configures the objects, offering reflection on the sentimental, emotional qualities jewellery and transitional love objects share.

Jewellery Art, which has a conceptual narrative enquiry at its core locates itself between discourses, that is, what is thought and said about the subject area itself, including the history of traditional jewellery design, and the world. The creators of such work are faced with a multiplicity of possible trajectories that have already been established by social consciousness and cultural production.

A different strategy, which is more concerned with the re-valuation of material qualities and their meanings, can be observed in Gabriela Felgenträger's Cupfragment, 2002. Here an everyday object has been 'de-constructed' and put to new use. What seems to be the shard of an ordinary cup is selected for

Jivan Astfalck, Siggi (Siegmund), transitional object no. 1, 2003, part of Love Zoo, 'Steiff' fabric dog from 1960s wearing earrings made of fine gold, 9 ct gold, sterling silver and tourmalines

Gabriela Felgenträger, Cupfragment, 2002

aesthetic reasons, beautifully crafted and made specifically so it can be worn as a ring. The investigation of the status and value of objects is a concern shared by most jewellery artists. Things, which we are familiar with, domestic or otherwise, and which often carry specific cultural meanings are taken out of their context, they are re-assembled, re-contextualised and re-interpreted. This is nowhere as obvious as in the spectacular Mercedes project, 2001, by Ted Noten. A Mercedes has status value, which is recognised across the world; to take such a car apart to make brooches from it is an act of knowing re-configuration of value. The brooches by Noten are minimalist, highly wearable and crafted with great skill. They are successful jewellery pieces in their own right; to know where they came from adds another level of interpretative meaning to the work, since it subverts value hierarchies and undermines conventional understanding of materialistic status.

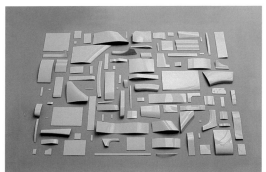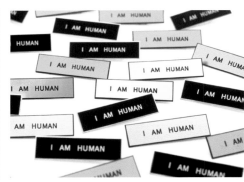

Similar dynamics can be observed where jewellery work turns its attention to the body itself. It is important to point out that all Jewellery Art implies the body, but some work is specifically focused on enquiries around the body, real or as a culturally formulated idea. Along with all the internal complexity of the work, the makers are faced with the multiple layers, and confusion, of meanings surrounding the body. This is well expressed by Auli Laitinen's I am Human brooches, 2000. The brooches are made from common office labelling equipment and offer no material value or skill-based surprises in themselves. We usually experience people wearing such name badges where the attempt to personalise human interaction should be helped by such 'body-signs'. In an almost cynical contradiction to their primary aim these labels are used in work environments, which usually are not concerned with individualised needs or subjective creativity; the badges signify their wearer as social bodies. Auli Laitinen's brooches, which read "I am Human", capture this complex dynamic; instead of individual names we read a much deeper, if not surreal, cry for recognition.

Ted Noten, Mercedes, brooches cut out of Mercedes-Benz, 2001, at Gallery Louise Smit, Amsterdam

Auli Laitinen, I am Human brooches, 2000, mixed media, photography: Gunnar Bergkrantz

What is achieved by the controlled introduction of text in Laitinen's work is accomplished in Gabriela Felgenträger's Sternum, 2003, by the juxtaposition of materials and suggested imagery. The plastic tubing used in the jewellery pieces is the clinically approved material used in surgery. Unless one is medically trained one would not know how this material — which eventually exists inside bodies — looks like, let alone know that it has aesthetic qualities. Felgenträger combined the pink tubing with silver castings of tree twigs, suggesting affinity of mater and passing comment on the ambivalence of notions like the natural and the artificial; notions, which become increasingly ambivalent and trigger more and more complex ethical debates.

The use of visual metaphors in such work achieves the construction of subjective meaning and can be regarded as a total re-evaluation and a re-description of reality; it allows for intervention and discovery. This is similar to the operation of metaphor in language, where the metaphorical quality allows the image to give body, shape, contour to meaning and furthermore, actually participates in the invention of meaning. New meanings emerge with the introduction of new metaphors. In this respect, the metaphorical quality of an object can be used as a device. A metaphor, in short, tells us something new about reality. This to me implies that innovation and the all-important shift in the status of the work can be obtained through the metaphorical 'twist' in the object or the discourse around the work. Jewellery Art has the capacity to deal with complex ideas whose components are derived from simpler images or previous experience, which are then combined in new and unexpected ways. They derive from a shift in the referential status, which takes place in the transition of the image as replica to the image as fiction. The new combination might have no reference to the previous original from which the image could be directly taken or copied.

Human life itself is organised by behaviour and cognition, it is already infused by value systems and worldviews at the point where it is transformed into an artistic structure. Art then, in my way of thinking, is the transformation of this pre-organised material into a new system and in doing so marks new values. When looking at Jewellery Art it remains to be important to remember that behind each created object stands a 'speaking person', who is constantly involved in dialogue with the world around him/herself. The objects, like speech or written text, are always socially charged and thus necessarily 'polemical'. Jewellery Art, because of its intimate relationship to the physical and cultured body, is perfectly placed to explore and communicate the nature of our

1 Gabriela Felgenträger,
   Sternum, from the series
2 Artificial limb, 2003, silver
   and tubing, 30 x 1.6 cm,
   photography:
3 Ralph Klein, Cologne

Gabriela Felgenträger,
from the series
Artificial limb, 2003,
silver and tubing,
photography:
Ralph Klein, Cologne

Eija Mustonen, Big Heart,
pendant, 1990,
electroformed copper

conflicted existence, as well as the pleasure we take in being alive. What is required in a sense is that we, as jewellery artists, explore the multitude of possibilities, each possibility a new aspect of understanding, each possibility providing a re-description, a new metaphor — to quote Jean-Luc Nancy:

… one must think the thought of the body thus. A double genitive: the thought that is the body itself, and the thought we think, we seek to think, on the subject of the body. This body here — mine, yours — which attempts to think the body and where the body attempts to be thought, cannot do so rigorously. That is, it cannot give up signifying the body, assigning signs to it — except by allowing itself to be brought back to its own thinking matter, to the very place from which it thoughtlessly springs.[1]

1. Nancy, J-L, "Corpus", Thinking Bodies, Flower MacCannell, J and Zakarin, L eds., Stanford, CA: Stanford University Press, 1994, p. 27.

A PART / APART

Caroline Broadhead

Contemporary jewellery has long sloughed off the assumed connotations of wealth, luxury, durability and privilege, concentrating instead on investigations into material, form, value, colour and movement. This edging out from tradition has meant that ideas have inevitably converged with those originating from other disciplines, notably fine art, and the exploratory nature of contemporary art practice has resulted in work that overlaps with other areas.

It is difficult to find the right word to describe this hybrid work. The word jewellery is inaccurate. Most contemporary jewellery does not include jewels as such and while other attempts to describe this work have been tried such as accessories, body decoration or body adornment, these do not either give enough consideration to the role of the object itself, or do not encompass the fundamental ideas that the relationship between the body and an object can explore. It is a strand of work that centres on these issues that I will write about.

When objects are active at the boundary of the body – jewellery in its widest sense – there is the potential to explore identity and meaning. Wearing something close to the body offers the circumstances and territory to explore issues that arise at this junction of the personal, social and cultural. Objects that are used in a close relationship to an individual can indicate a personal history, declare a relationship to others, and raise issues of identity and status. What is worn is a source of constant fascination and curiosity, demonstrating the continual two-way process of expression by one person and the impression it makes upon others. This essay will look at examples of work from the disciplines of jewellery, sculpture and video that operate at and question that boundary, and that demonstrate how an object might merge or be in confusion with the body.

Mona Hatoum's Hair Necklace, 1995, and Nanna Melland's Dekadence, 2003, use material from the artists' own bodies, exploring what was once self and what is now not, both a part of, and apart from the body. The change in affection for

Mona Hatoum, Hair Necklace, 1995, artist's hair, Cartier bust and leather, 31 x 22 x 17 cm, edition of 3, © the artist, courtesy Jay Jopling/ White Cube (London), photography: Edward Woodman

Nanna Melland, Dekadence, 2003, 750 gold and linen, 21 cm, Gallery Marzee, Neijimgen, The Netherlands

Janine Antoni, Ingrown,
1998, C-print, edition of 8,
41 x 46 cm, courtesy the
artist and Luhring Augustine,
New York

these materials when they are no longer part of the body, as they become waste, is acute. Nails and hair require continual grooming and when cared for, are a point of pride and power, but when separated and discarded from the body are seen to be 'other', and somehow offensive. They still belong, but are no longer owned, both anonymous and highly personal. Hair and nails operate on a slightly different timescale than the rest of the body, both lagging behind, continuing to grow after the body has died and surviving long after the rest of the body has perished. The transformation of these bodily materials into objects that are then to be placed back onto the body raises issues of mortality and of defining the elusive and ever changing boundary of a person.

Mona Hatoum's Hair Necklace takes the form of a string of beads. The way the beads are graded in size and weight to hang towards the front and the system of display reinforces certain traditional qualities of elegance and refinement. Attraction is quickly succeeded by repulsion, the familiarity and the status quo of this image immediately countered by a physical response to the idea of someone else's hair touching the skin. Nanna Melland's piece represents one year's worth of the trimmings of her nails, documenting the time taken to grow and collect. These are cast in gold, a material unchanged by time, and so, the discarded becomes iconised, the trivial becomes grand. Animal claws have been used in jewellery as talisman or trophies, showing superiority over another creature, these, in contrast, make a memento of the mundane routine of personal care.

The less practical care of nails is the shaping, the painting, the beautifying. The extent to which women go in the pursuit of beauty and allure is exaggerated and the constraints these conventions impose are dramatised in Janine Antoni's photograph, Ingrown, 1998. Usually false nails are used to imitate and become part of the body; here, the false nails have taken control, so instead of ten nails there are only five, with each end having a finger attached, linking pairs of fingers together. Red and polished, they indicate a classic ideal of leisure, elegance and seduction but also force the hands into a gesture of emptiness and a self-imposed helplessness. The title Ingrown suggests the body acting against itself, causing pain and discomfort.

Like Antoni's, Millie Cullivan's lace collar is a momentary work made lasting by the photograph. Made in 2004, an image is traced onto the bare skin with white dust. Transient, feminine, tender, what's left behind is a memory of touch, evidence of contact with the skin. There is an illusion of substance, but on recognition of its ephemerality, almost a holding of one's breath so as not to disturb the image. The human body is constantly regenerating itself and this process entails a person shedding thousands of microscopic particles every minute. A body is involuntarily and gradually dispersed into the immediate environment, in an almost negligible way. In Linsey Bell's Dust Interaction II, 2004, this process is recorded to reveal it as delicate, romantic and beautiful. Particles of human dust are captured by the use of strong light against a dark background as they are blown from the body. This dust, or dirt, can be classified as matter out of place, and as Mary Douglas in her book Purity and Danger explains: "Reflection on dirt involves reflection on the relation of order to disorder, being and non being, form to formlessness, life to death."[1]

 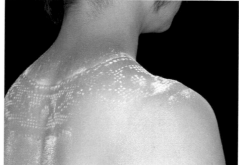

Cornelia Parker evokes ideas of communication and connection with the piece, The Negative of Whispers, ear plugs made from fluff gathered in the Whispering Gallery, St Paul's Cathedral, London, 1997. The title animates our thoughts about the fluff, or dust, which we now imagine has participated in or been witness to secrets and whisperings. The dust which has eavesdropped upon and absorbed confidences or rumours is now returned to the body's place of hearing — the ears, and itself becomes an impediment to hearing. Dust and the sense of order and disorder that comes with it, reminds us of the process of selection by which we guard the body's boundaries, allowing certain materials to touch or to enter the openings of the body and not allowing others, areas of the body that are more at risk of contamination than others.

In works by Guiseppe Penone and Gillian Wearing, the act of looking is examined by obstructing what is usually on view. The means by which we relate and communicate to another person is interrupted. In Penone's Rovesciare i propri occhi (To reverse one's eyes), 1970, mirror contact lenses arrest the movement

Linsey Bell, Dust Interaction II, 2004

Millie Cullivan, lace collar, 2004

Guiseppe Penone,
Rovesciare i propri occhi
(To reverse one's eyes),
1970, photography: Paolo
Mussat Sartor

Naomi Filmer, mouthpiece,
1996, photography:
Gavin Fernandes

of looks passing between two people, sealing the wearer off, breaking his gaze, and bouncing back the view that the wearer would be otherwise be seeing. Interfering with ordinary eye-to-eye communication, the gaze rests on the surface of the eye, the edge of the body and then sees only him or herself, albeit in a miniature and distorted way. Contact lenses, the means of being able to see clearly are now tiny masks that confound both inward and outward looking. In Wearing's Self Portrait, 2000, what is hidden in Penone's piece is revealed. This photograph is of Wearing wearing a mask of her own face, with only the eyes showing through, these become the point of reassurance in one's attempt to identify what is what in this mixture of real and representation. This mask does not hide identity, as the mask is a replica of Wearing's own face, it hides only expression. As with Hatoum and Melland's pieces, the ambiguity is in the combination of the living body and the lifeless. In other pieces, Trauma, 1994, and Confess all on video. Don't worry you will be in disguise. Intrigued?, 1994, Wearing uses the anonymity and protection that masks give, so that the participants in the video feel able to communicate what they perceive to be socially unacceptable information. The masks in these series allow secrets, truth, guilt or shame to be shared, explored and broadcast. In Trauma, Wearing used masks of juvenile faces to disguise the people relating their traumatic experiences. The masks cover up any possible signs of emotional damage on their real faces and so serve as the reminder of a more innocent past, a positive memorial, a clean starting point.

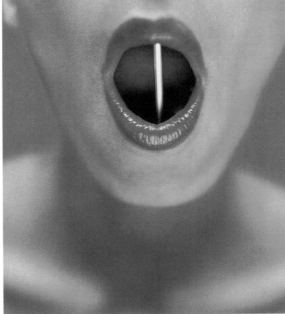

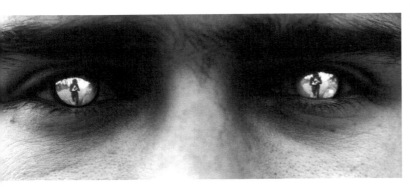

Wearing's masks allow people to speak freely from behind a façade. In contrast, the title of Lesley Vik's Scold's Bridle, 1998, refers to the role of an object where the behaviour, the speech, of one person could be dominated and controlled by another. Scold's bridles were metal bits inhibiting speech used by men on their wives, if they were considered to be talking too much. Vik's bridle is a piece that is held in the mouth voluntarily. This piece communicates an inability to speak verbally, whilst also conveying an expression through materials and visual image of the combination of beauty and restraint. Recently, the mouth, a highly erotic, sensual and intimate part of the body where we speak, eat, swallow, lick, suck, spit and kiss, has become an area for exploring objects

 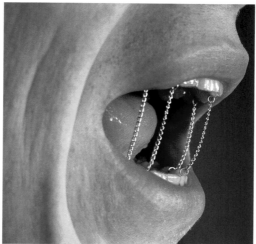

that can be seen to be both inside and outside the body. Like Vik's, Naomi Filmer's mouthpiece, 1996, made for Hussein Chalayan, is a mixture of intrigue, discomfort, and a sense of invasiveness. It is a silver strut holding the mouth open, making the inside more visible. This position becomes unnatural when maintained over a duration of time, making it impossible to swallow or speak. The idea of drawing attention to the inside of the mouth is also apparent in Craig Isaac's Superfluous Appliances, 1998. Aware of a trend to wear braces to enhance appearance rather than for orthodontic purposes, Isaac made pieces that cover the teeth with colours, text or decorations and without an obvious function. In one, the upper set of teeth are connected to the lower ones with fine silver chains which appear as a trace of spittle from a tender or aggressive act. Shinichiro Kobayashi in Point of contact (kiss), 1993, describes the sensation of intimacy and touch, by making a cast of two people kissing. By recording and

Lesley Vik, Scold's Bridle, 1998

Craig Isaac, Superfluous Appliances, 1998

translating the physical space that defines two people as close, but separate beings, the experience of a kiss becomes a visible and tangible, but visually unrecognisable, object.

The boundary of a person can be defined or brought into question in relationships with others. Laura Potter's Joint Custody, 2003, represents a relationship of a different kind. It masquerades as a mass-produced chain necklace bearing a stereotyped identity with the word "Mum" on one end and "Dad" on the other, to be twisted round to read the appropriate name at the front. The fact that it is one necklace and not two, shows the down to earth versatility that is called upon by children adapting to changing circumstances and relationships. The ability to conceal one allegiance and display another is a practical, but two-faced solution in uniting conflicts of interest.

Symbolic of the value of personal relationships, other traditional jewellery forms are also sites for the exploration of complex and ambiguous relationships in the modern world. By itself, the wedding ring has enough cultural tender to create narratives and elicit a wide variety of responses. Despite marriage's changing status, the wedding ring is still a piece of jewellery that performs at the intersection of personal aspirations and beliefs and the demands and expectations of society. The wedding, engagement and eternity ring are the most symbolic of jewellery pieces, tracking a conventional relationship from courtship to partners celebrating anniversaries, and incidentally, where design possibilities are most reduced. Two jewellers who have explored this iconography are Otto Künzli and Gerd Rothmann, both of whom have been in the forefront of contemporary European jewellery for many years and have consistently produced work investigating the nature of jewellery at its most essential.

Laura Potter,
Joint Custody, necklace,
2003, 9 ct gold, length
name to name 40 cm,
photography: L Cheung

Otto Künzli, Chain,
1985-1986, gold,
length 85 cm,
photography: Otto Künzli

For Chain, 1985–1986, Otto Künzli collected used wedding rings from people who responded to his newspaper advertisement to donate a wedding ring and tell its story. The history of each marriage was recorded and each of the 48 rings forms a link on the chain, superficially the same, but individual differences are quickly observed: small, thin, chunky, inscribed, plain. The rings have witnessed the promises made and subsequent lives lived; some are harmonious, some dramatic, poignant or tragic. They are now linked to each other, implying a repetitive and collective chain of events, and all contribute their share of emotional weight to the piece. Gerd Rothmann's Married – Engaged – 18th Birthday, 1992, presents the finger as part of the ring, or vice versa, both of which have grown together and are inseparable. Only the outer side of the ring and finger is existent, what a casual viewer would see on someone else's hand, with no means of staying on a finger. Mask-like, they are preserved in a jewellery box, like precious relics. Another piece by Künzli, Ring for Two People, 1980, links two people together, side by side, making literal the wedding ring symbolism of two people being joined as one. There is a humour in the unworkability of this piece, but also, a very particular view of the partnership. The particular distance between them is rigid and nonnegotiable. The couple's slight difference in height is not accommodated. There is an element of discomfort and restriction implied by the lack of easy movement. In contrast, Lin Cheung's How Long is a Piece of String?, 1997, is delicate and mobile, a more flexible arrangement, a greater distance between the two is allowed, but still measured. The piece is made up of two rings, worn by two people and joined by a length of gold wire stretched to its finest possible dimension, suggesting the limit of how far away one might go before the connection is broken. It acts as a reminder of how fragile that connection may be, what care needs to be taken to keep the relationship intact.

Lin Cheung, How Long is a Piece of String?, 1997, photography: Frank Thurston

Gerd Rothmann, Married – Engaged – 18th Birthday, models, 1992, three rings, silver, gold-plated, casket: 7 x 19 x 4 cm

Otto Künzli, Ring for Two, 1980, stainless steel, 2.1 x 12.3 x 0.25 cm, photography: Otto Künzli

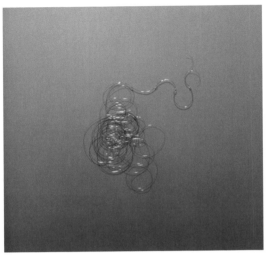

Cornelia Parker, Suit, Shot
by a Pearl Necklace and
Dress, Shot with Small
Change (Contents of a
Pocket), 1995, courtesy
Frith Street Gallery,
London

Cornelia Parker, Wedding
Ring Drawing
(circumference of a living
room), 1996, courtesy
Frith Street Gallery,
London

The idea of the pair and the malleability of gold are used in Cornelia Parker's
Wedding Ring Drawing (circumference of a living room), 1996, which re-forms
two wedding rings. The resulting length of gold thread creates an image of
the space where this relationship might develop. It marks out the perimeter
of a living room, like the rope around a boxing ring, a confined space where
intimacies of domestic life are played out. A gendered pair of objects also
figures in Parker's pair of works, Suit, Shot by a Pearl Necklace and Dress, Shot
with Small Change (Contents of a Pocket), from 1995. The pearls and small
change, the very reason why these clothes are capturing our interest, are absent.
What remains is the damage they have done. Pearls, for the most part, are
understood to be establishment jewellery, these, and the insignificant coins left
in a pocket form incongruous ammunition. Missing and loose fibres round the
wounds are, on the one hand, evidence of an act of violence, a disruption of
these socially respectable clothes, but they also focus attention in the same way
a piece of jewellery would. Deterioration of what is worn close to the body
points to "a concept of time as otherness that at once pertains to and disrupts
the self. Like pearls shooting through the suit, time penetrates the very texture
of the self and yet remains inassimilable."[2]

Layers of clothes are permeable boundaries of the body and, here, the holes
have greater importance than the garment itself, as they are the means of
passage between inside and out. Susanne Hammer's Orientierungshilfen, 1998,
maps the distinguishing marks of the body — the moles. This is a T-shirt whose
holes are made-to-measure, framing and presenting one person's unique

features, mapping their uniqueness. This piece focuses on the way the inside reveals itself on the skin, whereas a similarly structured piece by Sarah Lucas suggests the opposite direction, attention from the outside moving inward. Her large photographic print, Priere de Toucher, (Please touch), 2000, was installed in the Freud Museum, London in an exhibition called Beyond the Pleasure Principle. A hole in the T-shirt is aligned with the nipple, both concentrating attention there and also limiting accessibility. It is both an invitation to touch, but by its seemingly incidental nature, also a disregard or denial of that invitation. This hint of transgression is reminiscent of the film The Piano, when Harvey Kietel's character touches Holly Hunter's leg through a hole in her stocking, creating a subtle, highly charged sense of the erotic.

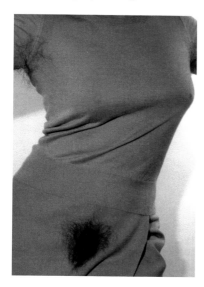 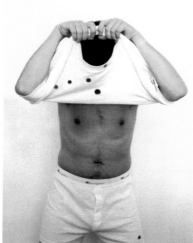

In Adele Lutz's Venus Twist, 2001, the body itself appears to grow outwards through the clothes. Body hair surfaces through the skirt and jersey to show underarm and pubic hair, the garments are no longer protection of privacy, they merge with the body to become one and the same. The soft beige colour and quality of the outfit indicate a self control, a sophistication and a certain position within society, while the hair of the sexual body demands our attention, trespassing onto the territory of the social body.

Social behaviour is shown by what we wear and what we eat: both are questions of taste and are signs that are interpreted by others. In Bobby Baker's Displaying the Sunday Dinner, 1998, what is destined to be inside the body is presented on

Adele Lutz,
Venus Twist, 2001,
photography:
David Byrne

Susanne Hammer,
Orientierungshilfen, 1998

the outside. The ritual of preparing and presenting food for a family or guests becomes part of a bizarre folk costume. The estrangement of food from its usual function by its positioning on the body also figures in Erwin Wurm's work. His series Outdoor Sculptures Taipei, 2000, photographs situations where nonchalant people assume unlikely positions with everyday objects. There is an absurdity in the way objects support, fit, balance on parts of the body or connect people, who seem to be responding to a silent or unknown challenge. In one, a woman is seen through a car window unselfconsciously wearing mushrooms wedged into her nostrils. Each attempt to form an interpretation of this image raises more uncertainties. Baker's and, in particular, Wurm's works show us a situation where a person defines him or herself as a separate, individual being, in a private world with a logic that is convincing from the inside and strange from the outside. Kate Bush writes of a related work, One Minute Sculptures, "Erwin Wurm points to the awkwardness and limits of the human body in relation to the things which surround it."[3]

1 2

Bobby Baker, Displaying the Sunday Dinner, 1998, photography: Andrew Whittuck

Erwin Wurm, Outdoor Sculptures Taipei, 2000, C-print, 126.5 x 159.1 cm, courtesy Galerie Nicola von Senger, Zurich

All the artists discussed in this essay use the direct experience of wearing or placing something on the body, bringing a sense of touch and intimacy into play. Positioning objects close to the body engages complex sensibilities in both the wearer and the audience prompting empathetic and objective responses simultaneously. The body is a necessary pre-condition for these works, and all refer to the way a person can be defined. The boundary of an individual is not a precise one, and it is in this intangible zone that these works operate. Each work offers a reflection on the potential for an object to merge with or to become confused with a person. The physical boundary is explored in the use of hair, nails and human particles, the materials that declare their previous state of being a part of the body. The concern, of mapping the distinguishing marks of an individual, is one of defining what is one and not another. Objects that affect or control the body's movement interfere with the wearer's autonomy, and therefore with their definition as a person. In the examples of Gillian Wearing's work, the use of masks gives an opportunity for a psychological boundary to alter. A definition is also formed by relationships with others, demonstrated by conventional means, such as the wedding ring, or Sarah Lucas's hole in the T-shirt. A boundary of a person can be identified from both directions, from within, by the individual and from without, by others. Fields of jewellery, fine art and fashion overlap in their examination, through objects, of this liminal space at the boundary of the body.

1. Douglas, Mary, Purity and Danger, London: Routledge, Kegan and Paul, 1966, p. 5.
2. Lajer-Burcharth, Ewa in Iwona Blazwick et al, Cornelia Parker, Turin: Hopefulmonster, 2001, p. 80.
3. Bush, Kate, Erwin Wurm, London: The Photographers Gallery, 2000, p. 3.

Jane Adam
Nana Akashi
Katie Clarke
Hilde De Decker
Nora Fok
Katy Hackney
Dorothy Hogg
Susan Kerr
Beth Legg
Kayo Saito
Mariana Sammartino
Charlotte De Syllas

ORGANIC FORMS

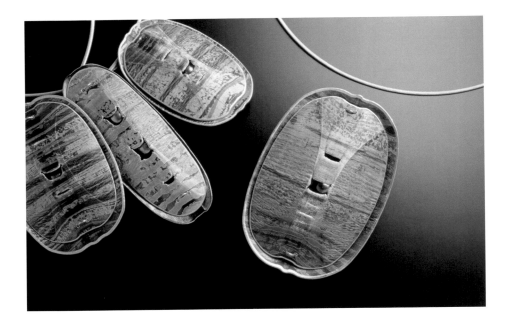

1	2
3	4

1 Oyster Brooch Pendants, 2004, anodised, dyed and textured aluminium, 9 ct gold, silver and freshwater pearls, average size 8.5 x 2.5 cm, photography: Joël Degen

2 91 Triangle Neckpiece, 2003, anodised, dyed and crazed aluminium, silver and stainless steel wire, length 56 cm, photography: Holly Jolliffe, model: Vibe Søndergaard

3 Corrugated Brooch, 2003, anodised, dyed and textured aluminium and stainless steel pin, 8.5 x 2.5 cm, photography: Joël Degen

4 Etched Brooches, 2002, anodised, etched, dyed and crazed aluminium, stainless steel and 9 ct gold, average length 7 cm, photography: Joël Degen

Jane Adam

Jane Adam's work is the result of over 20 years of experimenting with aluminium. This material, traditionally associated with industry, is transformed in Adam's innovative application of colour. The aluminium is anodised giving the metal a hard, transparent surface layer of aluminium oxide, which allows the absorption of dyes and inks which are applied using hand-printing techniques, creating layers of textured marks. Colours in Adam's work are subtle and diffused, with her palette of earthy complementary colours such as purple and yellow, red and green, along with the sensitive application of dyes, making her pieces highly painterly.

Etched Brooches, 2000-2002 are constructed as simple forms with unexpected hues and iridescence. These works are inspired by the textures and colours of bark and other plant life. The haphazard dispersal of colour on the aluminium echoes these organic forms, with the application of the dyes rendering each piece unique. In 91 Triangle Neckpiece, 2004, the surface of the small aluminium shards is almost pearlised, tinted with dusky purple, which makes the piece shimmer in the light. The construction of the neckpiece from the small pieces of aluminium has a surprising lightness, with the forms being suggestive of feathers. As the piece is worn, the small shards move and reflect the light, with the colours and textures subtly changing.

"By becoming part of the wearer's experience and expression, my work is transformed and completed."

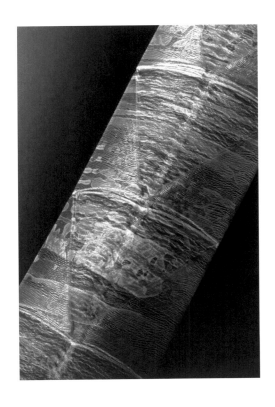

1	2	3
4	5	

1 Linked Necklace, 2000,
silver (cast) and cotton
flowers, each piece 2 cm,
photography: Nana Akashi,
model: Beth Gilmour

2 Bean, 2003, African
bean and silver (cast),
30 x 5 x 1 cm, photography:
Adrian Seah, model: Alice
Magnin

3 Chilli Whistle, 2003, silver
(cast), 13 x 1.5 x 1.5 cm,
photography: Adrian Seah,
model: Alice Magnin

4 Scales, 2001, tin and
silver, 15 x 15 x 20 cm,
photography: Nana Akashi,
model: Savitie Laopravatkul

5 Chilli Whistle, 2003, silver
(cast), 13 x 1.5 x 1.5 cm,
photography: Adrian Seah,
model: Alice Magnin

Nana Akashi

Nana Akashi's jewellery takes the forms of natural objects such as flowers, chillis and beans, and casts them in silver to make delicate and surprising pieces of jewellery. She believes that jewellery should stimulate the viewer's senses, incorporating movement and sound in her work, so that, for instance, her Linked Necklace, 2000, can be reconfigured with different elements such as jelly beans or feathers, as well as the length and sequence being flexible to suit the individual wearer. This interactivity is central to Akashi's method of working, considering not just the way her jewellery will look, but how it will affect the wearer, saying "I always look for possibilities beyond the beauty of my jewellery, and I will keep seeking these...."

Her Chilli Whistle, 2003, as implied by the title, continues this engagement with the function as well as the look of jewellery, with this piece being both a necklace and a musical instrument. When worn, the chilli is a pretty charm, which is then brought to life when raised to the lips. From the same collection, the oversized ring, Bean, 2003, rattles as it is moved on the viewer's finger, more like an object of entertainment than adornment. Akashi's jewellery, with its fragile appearance and unexpected transformations, echo the natural forms they are based on, free-associating around the wearer's senses of touch, sound and sight.

Katie Clarke

Katie Clarke's work is inspired by fly-fishing and the associated art of fly-tying — a tradition of using brightly coloured feathers on the fishing-line to attract fish. Experimenting with a broad range of materials, from crystal fibres and elastic, to more traditional components such as gold and silver, her elegantly futuristic pieces have been shown extensively nationally and internationally, as well as having been showcased in magazines ranging from The Face to New York's Paper.

Using the feather as her design source, Clarke transforms it from a soft organic form into a multiplicity of geometric units that radiate out from the main base, be it a ring, necklace or earring. Her design ethos is rooted in material experimentation, with a profound interest in the combinations of colours as well as a sophisticated manipulation of rhythm, form, and texture. In many of her pieces she combines the form and feeling of feathers with the hardness and sheen more associated with insects, creating a symbolic and material tension in her work, with the pieces evoking both a play of refined carapace-like surfaces and a brilliant display of ethereal hues. This oscillation from hard to soft, from complex to bold, and from experimental to wearable shows her work to be embedded in a tradition of innovation and stylish practicality.

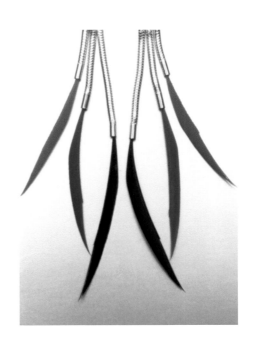

1 Blue Double Spikey Round Ring, 2000, feather and silver, 5 x 4 cm

2 Sea Urchin Ring, 2002, feather and silver, 5 x 4 cm

3 Cage Choker and Bracelet, 2002, feather and silver, choker 32 x 5 cm, bracelet 15 x 5 cm

4 Three Tier Snake Chain Earrings, 2002, feather and silver, 10 cm

photography:
Sophie Broadbridge

1 Greenhouse, 2004

2 For the farmer and market gardener, 1999, tomato and gold ring

3 For the farmer and market gardener, 2004, white aubergine and found ring

4 For the farmer and market gardener, 2004, purple aubergine and silver ring

5 For the farmer and market gardener, 2004, pepper and found ring

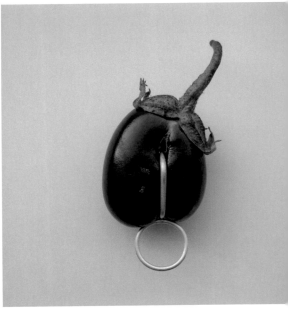

Hilde De Decker

Hilde De Decker pushes jewellery's function and context to the limits, playing with materials, techniques and appearances. For instance, she prefers white boiled silver to the classic high polished finish, and instead gives everyday items of tableware a lustrous surface, or as in her series Household Effects, 1997, copies abandoned objects such as can openers, coasters, biscuits or forks in precious materials.

In her series For the farmer and market gardener, 1999-2004, De Decker was influenced by the bizarre occurrence of a wedding ring turning up around a potato 20 years after it had been lost. Here it is the vegetable that 'wears' the jewellery or the other way around, where the jewellery wears the fruit. She presents a paprika with a bejewelled ring squeezed onto it as it grows, a purple aubergine or tomato pinched as in a stone setting, and explores unusual colours, textures and forms with the vegetables grown through and around the jewellery. In the installation of this work, De Decker constructed a greenhouse in a gallery and allowed the process of vegetable and metal intertwining to take place before visitors' eyes.

Nora Fok

Nora Fok works mainly with nylon monofilament to create what she calls "wearable sculptural objects". She uses techniques normally associated with the manipulation of yarn: knitting, knotting, tying, weaving and plaiting, occasionally incorporating plastic and other materials into the pieces. Her jewellery is very much based on the organic fluidity of life, as she says: "The idea that heaven, earth and man should coexist in harmony is in Chinese philosophy, and also plays an important part in the creative inspiration for my jewellery."

Nora Fok is best known for her Bubble Bath Series, which was made especially for an exhibition and educational project, Thirteen Hands, curated by children for children. This exhibition was launched in 2001 at the Inverness Museum and Art Gallery and toured Britain. "I think the children chose my work because of the material I use. All my jewellery pieces have a story to tell and it is colourful and fun." Bubble forms are created from white opaque nylon thread conjuring up the image of foaming soap. The bubbles' transitory quality is captured in the intricate and effervescent nature of these works which include neckpieces and bracelets.

Calculator, 2002, is a large neckpiece based on an abacus. Taking inspiration from this ancient calculating device, the piece is nevertheless organic and flamboyant. "By changing the rectangular shape to the circular form it became a wearable piece of sculpture," says Fok. Woven nylon forms a ribbed undulating sphere around which the baubles can be adjusted, fully functioning as an abacus, if desired. Recalling the shape and size of Elizabethan collars, Fok describes the work as "glamour with a touch of humour".

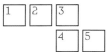

1 Bubble Bath Bracelet, 2001, knitted clear nylon, 22 cm, photography: Frank Hills, model: Nora Fok

2 Bubble Bath Neckpiece, 2001, knitted clear nylon, 45 cm, photography: Frank Hills, model: Nora Fok

3 Fountain Neckpiece, 2004, bearded dyed nylon with black pearls, 38 cm diameter, photography: Holly Jolliffe, model: Emie Elg

4 Calculator, 2002, woven, knitted clear and pigmented nylon, 65 cm diameter, photography: Holly Jolliffe, model: Emie Elg

5 Tumbleweed Ring, 1999, knitted, tied and woven clear and pigmented nylon with gold leaf, 8 cm, photography: Holly Jolliffe

Katy Hackney

"I like to use unusual materials in my work."

Katy Hackney uses materials that are more normally associated with the mundane, practical objects that surround us such as cellulose acetate which is used for spectacles and cutlery handles. A key element in her designs, fragments of vintage patterned Formica, come from her searches in hardware stores or junkshops, with only random small chips being available, determining the look of each piece. She has said about this process that "this makes it more precious, with only a tiny amount available for my use, each piece is unique, the pattern inspiring my design". In many of Hackney's pieces plywood is also incorporated, playing on the original use of Formica as a worktop surface, along with silver which is riveted to the surface of brooches, giving these practical materials an appearance of gemstones or precious materials.

Hackney gathers much of her inspiration from ceramic and textile design, especially from the 1950s and 1960s. This is clear from the pastel and primary colours used, the playful nature of the work and simplified shapes. The bold design of Twig and Leaf Bracelet, 2003, transforms the natural source material with a quality reminiscent of illustrations from children's books. Her rings seem carved out from another era — stacked on plywood platforms sits a feast of vibrant colour and pattern.

1 Twig and Leaf Bracelet, 2003, cellulose acetate and silver, 18 x 7 x 0.6 cm, photography: Katy Hackney

2 Brooch with Sprout, 2004, vintage Formica, plywood, silver, paint, steel and varnish, 5 x 5 x 1.4 cm, photography: Graham Murrell

3 Brooch with 2 Plants, 2004, vintage Formica, plywood, silver, steel and varnish, 7 x 6 x 1 cm, photography: Graham Murrell

4 Nature Necklace, 2004, vintage Formica and oxidised silver, 70 x 3 cm, photography: Katy Hackney

5 Sets of Rings, 2004, vintage Formica, plywood and silver, 3.5 cm high, photography: Graham Murrell

Dorothy Hogg

As sculptor and jeweller Dorothy Hogg invites us to both enjoy observing her work and wearing it. Both austere and opulent, Hogg's jewellery evokes the style of Art Deco, with the space and decoration of the Mackintosh building at the Glasgow School of Art where she studied being an early influence on her work. In the Artery Series, 2002-2004, fortified silver mingles with flashes of blood red, with the works appearing at first to be minimalist abstract designs. However, this recent series looks to the depths of the human body for inspiration, with the forms drawing on cells, platelets, veins, and the heart which are translated in metal, felt and coral. Hogg's work over the last three decades has constructed a vocabulary of subtle abstraction, with this series providing a new set of references. Other themes that have inspired Hogg include the idea of sound and movement, in pieces such as Noisy Necklace with Campanile Forms, 1999.

A formal quality of Hogg's work that is not immediately apparent is the lightness of her pieces. The silver is hollowed out by hand, so that the 'arteries' in her recent work are capable of transmitting fluid through the networks created. This attention to detail in her work points to the conceptual edge that sets her pieces apart from simple decoration.

"My aesthetic is driven by my subconscious mind and reflects in an abstract way events and changes in my life. The structure of the body, its movements and related conscious and unconscious symbolic thoughts preoccupy my design process."

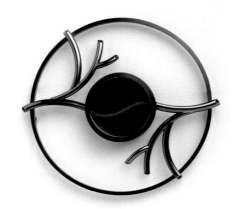

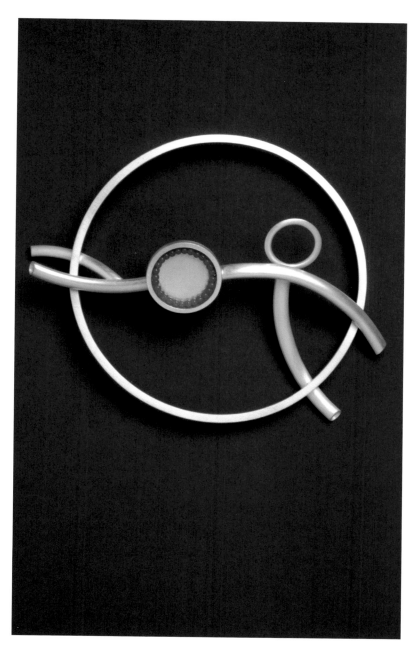

1 Artery Series Neckpiece,
2004, silver and red felt,
10 cm diameter

2 Artery Series Neckpiece,
2002, silver and red felt,
20 x 20 cm

3 Artery Series Brooches,
2003, silver and red felt,
8.5 and 10 cm long

4 Artery Series Brooch, 2004,
silver and coral, 11 x 8.5 cm

5 Artery Series Brooch, 2004,
oxidised silver and coral,
11 cm diameter

6 Artery Series Brooch, 2004,
oxidised silver and red felt,
11 cm diameter

Photography:
John K McGregor

1	2
3	4
	5

1 Deco Earrings, 2003, silver, oxidised silver and synthetic bead, length 7 cm, photography: B Kerr

2 Half Moon Brooch with Fuchsia, 2004, silver and leather, 7.2 x 2.8 cm, photography: L Watson

3 Petal Cup Studs, 2004, silver, various sizes, photography: B Kerr

4 Oval Pattern-Drop Earrings, 2003, silver, oxidised silver and leather, length 5.8 cm, photography: B Kerr

5 Miniature Brooches, 2004, silver and oxidised silver, 2 x 1.8 cm, photography: B Kerr

Susan Kerr

"The first thing that strikes you about Susan's work is that it's like being faced with an exquisite array of fine chocolates. Each one is tempting, sweet and so very dainty."
Ideas Factory, Channel 4 website

Flirtatious and fashion orientated, Susan Kerr's pieces are almost garments in themselves – with silver cut outs exposing internal layers of coloured leather. She uses leather dyed in vibrant hues, contrasting with the bold shapes of the silver, saying about her pieces: "I like the fact that I can change the whole style of a piece simply by changing the colour; from subtle grey, for example, to vibrant green. It also creates a sensual, textile element which softens the silver."

The development of Kerr's jewellery occurs through two main areas of research; the drawing, painting and collecting of flowers and images and observation of trends in design. Her delicate cut outs in pieces such as Miniature Brooches, 2004, reference petal shapes, but abstract the source to create an minimal aesthetic that is reflected across her work.

Beth Legg

"The effects the passage of time has on substances fascinate me....
We observe the time and ageing processes but ultimately have no
control over them."

Beth Legg's work is infused with the atmosphere of the Scottish
Highlands where she lives, with everyday natural phenomena such
as flocking starlings, movements of the marram grasses, and the
ebb and flow of the tide all being suggested in her work. In the
collection of brooches Tidelines and Testpieces, 2004, heather root
and twig are wrapped in silver, iron wire or brass to create objects
that appear to have been found rather than made.

Legg is fascinated by bleached wood, ageing stone and rusting metal
because they have been exposed to a variety of layered eroding
processes, something that she mirrors in her own production
techniques. She rolls, splits open, and hammers to create profoundly
'weathered' pieces, referencing an idea of 'origin', of returning a
finished piece to its source.

Her series of rings from 2004 appear to be abstracted forms, with
Legg's choice of display drawing on the natural influences that
inform the works. The photographs of these rings allow the viewer
to see the echoes of the natural shapes in the designs, with, for
example, feathers alongside the solid silver Peewit Rings.

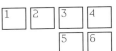

1 Flagstone Brooch, 2004,
Caithness flagstone and
sterling silver, 15 x 3 cm,
photography: Beth Legg

2 Tidelines and Testpieces,
2004, burnt heather root,
found twig, silver, iron wire
and brass, 14 x 7.5 cm,
7 x 1 cm and 6.5 x 2.5 cm,
photography: John K McGregor

3 Leather Split Rings, 2004,
sterling silver and leather,
0.09 cm gauge square
silver wire, photography:
John K McGregor

4 Filling and Found, rings,
2004, sterling silver and 18
ct yellow gold, 4 x 1.5 cm,
0.12 cm gauge wire,
photography: John K
McGregor

5 Peewit Rings, 2004,
oxidised silver, 0.12 cm
gauge wire, photography:
John K McGregor

6 Negative Form Rings, 2004,
oxidised sterling silver, 0.12
cm gauge silver wire,
photography: John K McGregor

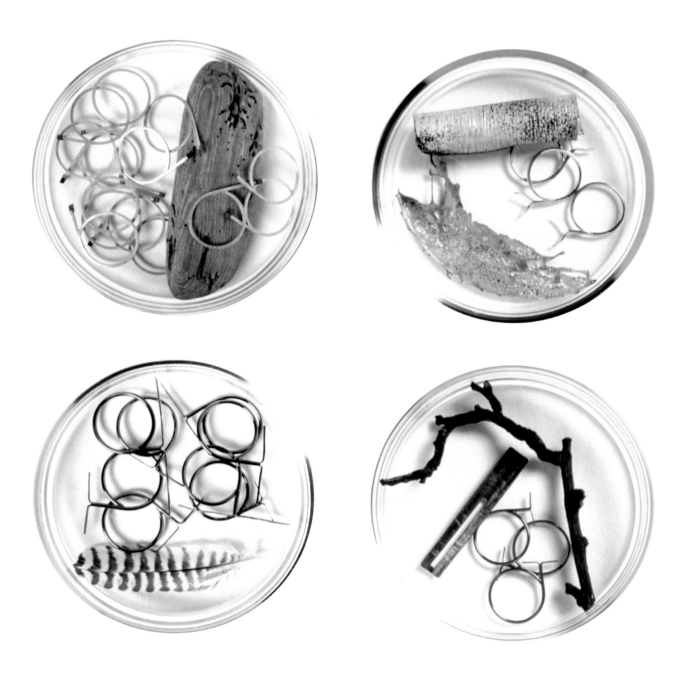

1 Summer Flower, 2004,
polyester fibre, freshwater
pearls and mono-filament
photography: Holly Jolliffe
model: Vibe Søndergaard

2 Rustling Brooches, 2002,
silver and magnets

3 Laurel Neckpiece, 2003,
polyester fibre, silver and
magnets

4 Layer Neckpiece and
Bracelet, 2002, polyester
fibre, silver, chrome wire
and magnets

Kayo Saito

"I regard my jewellery as a small sculpture that is complete on its own, as well as on the wearer's body."

Kayo Saito's work is based on the realm of nature, with what she calls its infinite potential for creativity. Saito carefully chooses materials to convey feelings of warmth and softness, in recent works using paper combined with polyester fibre to create delicate forms that look as if they have been grown onto their metal support. Often using magnets to fix the works in place, her signature circular forms echo the shapes of flower buds, with the long stems allowing for subtle movement that amplifies the origin of the work in natural world.

"My works are closely linked to the natural environment in which we live: plants and trees, their seasonal changes, rustling sounds, swaying movements and teeming vibrancy; shells and fossils; the colour and texture of these natural forms. After all, organic objects are the most beautiful crafted things in this world."

Mariana Sammartino

Mariana Sammartino uses stainless steel mesh and silver alongside gold or diamonds to create pieces that evoke the interplay, or in her words "the clashing and intersecting" of the natural and manmade world. The industrial material is moulded and reworked into organic undulating forms, with steel taking on the qualities of a delicate textile, often folded and thin, much like silk. As a material that is usually associated with large industrial structures, Sammartino is interested in the challenge that steel represents on this small scale, coming up with unconventional and technically demanding ways of holding, trapping and connecting the resulting mesh to silver or gold.

Having studied architecture and industrial design, it is clear that Sammartino is influenced by these disciplines, with City of Lights, 2004, being a brooch that recalls a network of roads and buildings as seen from the air, transformed into an organic undulation of folds and gems. Near the Equator, 2004, takes the shape of flower bulbs that are refigured so that the piece wraps around the neck rendering the body as part of flora, albeit with the texture and colour of an urban environment.

"I'm interested in exploring the dynamism of the subject matter relative to the moving path of the viewer. As one moves around the piece of jewellery, alternating volumes, intermittent splashes of brilliance, and periodic glances of iridescence are discovered. When the piece is worn the object, the body, the wearer and the observer begin a new transforming conversation."

1 Near the Equator, 2004,
stainless steel mesh
and sterling silver,
26 cm x 19 cm

2 Ascent, 2004,
stainless steel mesh and
sterling silver,
12.5 cm x 8 cm diameter

3 City of Lights, 2004,
stainless steel mesh,
sterling silver, 14 ct gold
and diamonds,
11 cm x 2.75 cm

4 Hydrozoan, 2004,
stainless steel mesh and
sterling silver,
10 cm x 11 cm diameter

6 Cruz Del Sur, 2004,
stainless steel mesh,
sterling silver,
14 ct gold and diamonds,
5.5 cm x 8 cm diameter

Charlotte De Syllas

Charlotte De Syllas works with gemstones, with her extensive experience in the field of stone carving coming through in the sculptural surfaces of her intricate pieces. Almost completely self-taught she has achieved an intimate knowledge of the extremes to which stone can be carved, inlaid and interlocked using a diamond tool. She has said: "The best and brightest colours that the earth possesses are my working materials. I have a passion for the qualities of stone and use metal only when really necessary".

De Syllas' pieces are theatrical, belying the natural source of much of her imagery. Tulip Ring, 2003, combines fuchsia tourmaline with 22 ct red gold, with the strong lines of the carving creating an almost abstract piece. Aquatic life is another source of imagery: shells, water, sea creatures and rocks are featured in, for example, Jellyfish Necklace, 2003, made from rock crystal and black jade. Over almost 40 years Charlotte De Syllas has been producing mainly one-off pieces, enjoying the challenge of creating jewellery to suit the character and features of the particular person, with her love of colour and form coming through in each piece.

1 Tulip Ring, 2003, red tourmaline and 22 ct red gold, top 3 x 3 cm, photography: Jasper Vaughan

2 Heliodor Ring, 2002, heliodor and 22 ct gold, top 3.5 x 1.5 cm, photography: David Cipps

3 Jellyfish Necklace, 2003, rock crystal, black jade, synthetic ruby and black gilt chain, 12 cm long and 3.5 cm wide, photography: David Cipps

4 Ceremonial Bracelet, 2000, black and white jade and white gold internal catch, 7.5 x 7 x 4 cm, photography: Ian Haigh

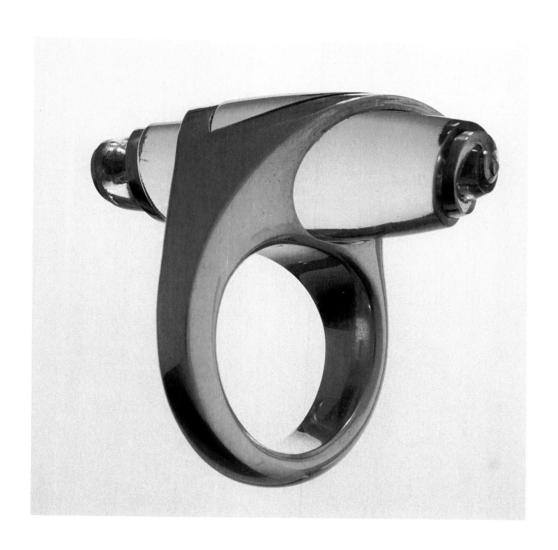

Victoria Archer
Gijs Bakker
Elizabeth Callinicos
Li-Sheng Cheng
Norman Cherry
Colette Hazelwood
Nanna Melland
Mike & Maaike
Mah Rana

SMALL STATEMENTS

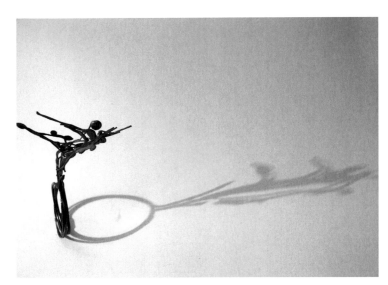

Victoria Archer

Victoria Archer's jewellery is characterised by a passion for illusion, movement and shadow. Using oxidised silver wire as her primary medium, Archer creates individually unique rings and headpieces that can be worn or displayed as sculpture and are always accompanied by a photograph of the worn object's cast shadow. She is fascinated by the way in which jewellery alters the contours of the body, extending it into the surrounding space. The impetus behind her practice is to create an adorned body that when seen in silhouette bears little resemblance to the original figure, with a parallel between Archer's aesthetic and that of the shadow sculptures of contemporary artists Tim Noble and Sue Webster wherein, for example, the cast shadow of a heap of trash approximates the New York skyline.

The shadows cast by the works in Archer's series of Rear Headpieces, 2004, create the illusion of a head with two profiles looking simultaneously in opposite directions. The sculptural forms of these pieces differ strikingly from the shadows they cast when worn. At first glance these works appear to be a chaotic array of curving metal twigs, wire mesh and other scraps, and it is only from their shadows that the structure of the headpieces emerges.

"Throughout history the body has been changed, distorted and exaggerated with the use of external structures. I'm interested in how the body can be changed, but also how someone could view the changed body as the real one without seeing the external structures."

1 Dancer Ring, 2004, oxidised silver

2 Rear Headpiece, 2004, oxidised silver

3 Rear Headpieces, 2004, exhibition display with silhouette photographs, dimensions variable

Gijs Bakker

Trained as a traditional jeweller, but equally at home in the respective fields of product, furniture design, and architectonics, Gijs Bakker brings an innovative use of materials and processes to the craft. Throughout his career as a designer and jeweller he has used unconventional materials, methods and subject matter, subverting the inherent value of precious medals and stones, and challenging the hands-on nature of craft.

In his series of Holysport brooches and pendants, 1998, he turns digitally manipulated photographs into three-dimensional products by using rapid prototyping and stereolithography. For Cellini with ball, 1998, Bakker uses the cut-out figure of Christ from a painting by Cellini. The figure balances on top of a football, sporting a T-shirt that has been pulled up over his head, a gesture mimicking that of a professional footballer who has just scored a goal. In all of the works in this series the iconography of Rennaissance painting is juxtaposed with the imagery of football, making a playful and ironic statement about the sport and how it is valued and considered heroic in our global culture today.

Using a similar technique and the same sense of irony, Bakker created an edition of brooches inspired by the slogan "I don't wear jewels, I drive them", from a car advertisement. For Jaguar 3E 1975, 2000, Bakker takes a photo of the front of jaguar car, sets it under plexiglass on top of a silver base and replaces the front windshield of the car with an amethyst stone. In this work, and others in the series, the surfaces of the car in the photograph are just as luminous and shiny as the jewels with which they are set.

1 Ferrari Dino 206 SP from the I don't wear jewels, I drive them series, 2001, opal, silver, photograph, and plexiglass, 5.9 x 7.5 x 3.9 cm

2 Cellini with ball from the Holysport series, 1998, white gold, silver, computer manipulated photograph, plexiglass, 11.3 x 9.3 x 5 cm

1 Silence is Golden, 2001,
18 ct yellow metal and
rubber, 6 x 2 cm

2 Price-less Tag, 2001/2004,
prototype made of silver,
4 x 2.5 cm

Elizabeth Callinicos

Elizabeth Callinicos uses her art practice to explore contemporary value systems. Starting from jewellery's traditional connotations of preciousness and prestige, Callinicos questions how we gauge the worth of people and their possessions.

Her piece entitled Price-less Tag, 2001/2004, a hand-made silver pendant in the shape of a pricetag, is designed to be worn. Callinicos' intention with this work is to point out that the value of an individual cannot be measured and that any means by which one might place a market value on human life is futile. She has made a series of these flat silver pricetags, each one made by hand despite the ease with which the simple form might be mass-produced. The effort imparted in the making of each one adds weight and meaning to the otherwise empty symbol of value, the blank pricetag, further emphasising the value of human labour and individuality.

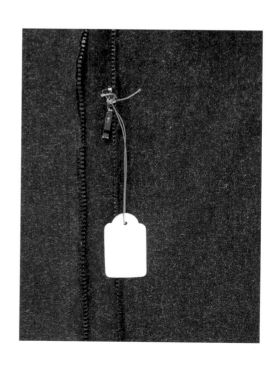

The work Silence is Golden, 2001, a brooch made of yellow metal and rubber with the word 'silence' cut out of it, is made to look like gold and carefully subverts the meaning of the old adage which makes up its title. By cutting out the word 'silence' and making its outline and absence out of faux-gold rather than the word itself, Callinicos implicitly tells us that she places greater value in communication (the lack of silence).

Li-Sheng Cheng

Li-Sheng Cheng's jewellery can only be fully understood and experienced when worn. In her Cycle rings, 2004, the cylindrical structure of the ring is made of silver whilst the inside, the part that touches the skin of the wearer, is covered with textured loofah or dotted with pearls. The outside remains either a simple smooth band or has protruding curves reflecting the inner life of the piece, the cavities that contain pearls that press against the wearer's fingers. Touch overrides sight in the perception these subtle works.

The wearer also plays a key role in Cheng's piece Transform, 2004, in that the shape of the ring dramatically changes when put on. In this piece the tiered silver ring is again lined with a textured material, however this time it is red felt that protrudes out of the ring in five spikes. When the ring is placed around the finger the spiky extensions separate.

The Transform ring's metamorphosis when worn approximates the organic growth present in Cheng's earlier work Eden Project Ring, 2001, in which a small glass globe encases a container of soil for a growing piece of grass. The connection between these two works highlights Cheng's intention to create jewellery with a life of its own.

"Objects have lives just like us. My intention is to create objects that possess lives and question the viewer's perception of them. Most of my work is in the form of containers, hiding symbolic elements of life, representing nerves or cells."

1 Transform, 2004, silver and felt, 2.5 x 9 cm

2 Cycle, 2004, pearls, silver and loofah, 2.6 x 2.3 cm, photography: Holly Jolliffe

3 The Eden Project Ring, 2001, grass, soil, glass and white metal, 6 x 4.5 cm (excluding length of grass)

Norman Cherry

Norman Cherry has invented Angiogenetic Body Adornment, 2004, a form of body modification that relies on biological engineering, the prototype for which has yet to be manufactured. Taking its name from 'angiogenesis', the natural process by which tissue is made, the 'jewellery' is constructed from the substance of the body itself. The process by which these body modifications are made is as follows: "Cells are cultured in vitro, then inserted into a biodegradable three-dimensional matrix of a given form which is reintroduced in corpo where the cells multiply and new tissue grows."

Cherry arrived at the idea for this type of adornment through his interest in the various methods by which people augment their bodies permanently, including tattooing, piercing, scarification and cosmetic surgery. He "explores the issues of conformity and inclusion, rejection and exclusion, individuality, intra and extra version".
His designs are informed by in-depth research into both historical and contemporary methodologies of body modification from various cultures. The flesh-made forms of Angiogenetic Body Adornment range from conventional jewellery shapes such as the circular loops of a bracelet that grow out from the wrist, to a linear pattern reminiscent of African scarification decorating the forehead.

1 Angiogenetic Body
Adornment, 2004, biologically
engineered tissue,
biodegradable matrix

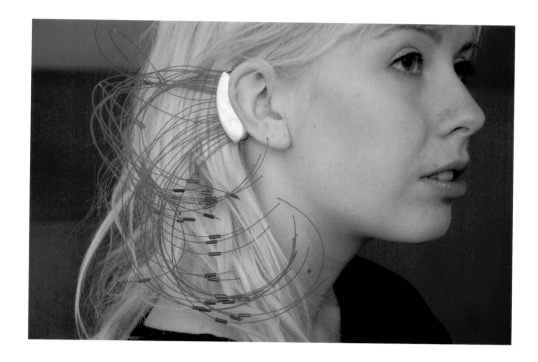

1 Hearing Aid Jewellery, 2002, silver and nylon, 9 x 4 cm, photography: Holly Jolliffe, model: Emie Elg

2 Squash the Gobstopper Mouthpiece, 2003, silver, 8 x 8 cm sphere

3 Squash the Gobstopper Mouthpiece, composite photograph, 2003

Colette Hazelwood

Colette Hazelwood develops her jewellery from a myriad of concepts and subject matter, defying simple definitions. In her recent work she explores the features of the face, the mouth and ears, as sites of both communication and ornamentation.

With her Hearing Aid Jewellery, 2002, Hazelwood celebrates the hearing aid by transforming these small medical items into striking fashion accessories. The normally skin-coloured hearing aid is covered and accentuated by a smooth silver curve mirroring the shape of the ear, with colourful nylon threads ornamented with beads protruding like hairs. Hazelwood overturns the negative associations that can accompany disability by adorning rather than hiding physical difference.

The reversal of meaning, employed in the Hearing Aid Jewellery with the turning a loss into a gain, is utilised in Squash the Gobstopper Mouthpiece, 2003, but in the opposite way. Although this work is constucted from the precious metal silver, it is not necessarily the kind of jewellery one would be flattered to receive, as it is designed to make the wearer mute. The silver globe engraved with political borders is to be placed in the mouth censoring speech, with the piece having been exhibited with a digitally manipulated photograph of George W Bush wearing it in his mouth, squashing the world with the power of his words.

Nanna Melland

Nanna Melland's jewellery questions the principles of decoration, pushing the boundary between ornamentation and art object. Working with corporeal elements such as a pig's heart and fingernails, body parts normally considered grotesque or unsightly, Melland creates precious objects of beauty addressing the sensitive subject of mortality.

For Heart Charm, 2000, Melland replaces the traditional polished metal heart of a charm bracelet with a visceral and fleshy pig's organ of the same name. The heart of a pig, chosen specifically for its likeness to a human heart, represents for Melland the most important life-giving part of the body. By replacing the heart, a symbol of love, with the literal organ, Melland dramatically alters the function of the bracelet and forces her viewer to confront the true meaning behind this symbol. This piece led to a series of work using pig's hearts. For her Fragments of Life brooches and pendants, 2003-2004, Melland cast the inside cavities of a pig's heart and placed the fragments within glass spheres that can be worn. These works further question the conventional heart form by replacing it with the innermost spaces of the internal organ.

"By bringing this hidden reality out into the light, the inner spaces of the heart, the invisible inner reality of us all which is so fantastic and fragile, I hope to make people contemplate what is difficult and unknown. To let them wonder and feel gratitude for their life, whatever it may look like."

1 Dekadence, 2003,
750 gold and linen, 21 cm

2 Heart Charm, 2000,
silver charm bracelet and
pig's heart

3 Fragment of Life II, 2004,
925 hallmarked silver, epoxy,
glass, pendant: 6.5 x 5 x
6.5 cm, chain: 38 cm

1 Shurtape, 2001, tape,
thread and wire,
16 x 29 x 5 cm

2 Rock Paper Scissors, 2001,
plastic, rock: 2.3 x 3.2 x
1.5 cm, paper: 2.8 x 4 x 8 cm,
scissors: 2.3 x 3.5 x 1 cm

3 Anti War Medal, 2003,
silver and yarn,
12 x 19 x 4 cm

Mike & Maaike

Mike Simonian and Maaike Evers designed their metal peace symbol brooch entitled Anti War Medal, 2003, as a response to the second US-lead war in Iraq. The brooch can be worn to form a coherent peace symbol displaying proudly the wearer's political opinion, or alternatively the four pieces can be pinned in a random manner as a private message to those in the know. Titled using the word 'medal' and taking the form of a brooch, the object mirrors the badges awarded soldiers for their duties in the battlefield, however this pendant is to "commemorate the courage to prevent" rather than implement violence, and is to be given to the millions who have protested and rallied against war.

On the more playful side, with Rock Paper Scissors, 2001, Simonian and Evers take the familiar symbols of the title's game to construct a unique, sleek set of plastic rings. Playing on the colloquial term 'rock' for the stone on a ring, the first of the three is a simplified shape of a traditional ring, with an elevated globe extending from the simple band. The other two forms — paper and scissors — are also simplified, with the three rings designed to interconnect two at a time to each other, just as two hands representing the signs interact in playing the game. As with the Anti War Medal, each piece of this set can be worn separately, but the whole is greater than the sum of its parts.

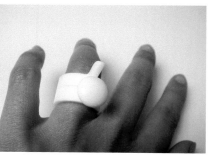

Mah Rana

Mah Rana's oeuvre is concerned first and foremost with the personal and communal significance of jewellery. For Rana, jewellery is a memento of personal history, it can be made of any material as long as its quintessential function is to assist memory. Take for example her work Out of the Dark, 2001-2002, a series of brooches to be worn when in mourning. The black textured surfaces of the discs slowly wear off, revealing the gold beneath and marking the passage of time. They serve to remind the wearer of their loss but also mark the stages of mourning from grief to acceptance with its physical transformation from darkness to light. The permanence of gold then serves as a life-long reminder of the lost loved-one.

Rana's necklace Toknot, 2002, is a testament to the anachronistic method of remembering by simply tying a knot. In Rana's words: "Toknot keeps memories I have of tying these knots, almost as if tying a knot would seal actual experience in my head. Sounds, colours and smells as well as conscious and subconscious feelings from that time openly come back to me when I look at the piece as if it were able to refocus my thoughts and take me back to the past or bring the past back into the present."

For Zodiac, 2002, Rana selected 12 found objects for the way in which their individual qualities complimented one another. Rana's intention was "to create an 'open system' that was free from existing rules and to offer the recipient their own meaning and importance to an object". For Rana, jewellery itself is 'an open system' of objects imparted with meaning and value only through subjective attachments and associations.

1 Zodiac, 2002, gold and found objects, dimensions variable

2 His 'n Hers, 1995/2002, gold (two used wedding rings), 2.1 x 6.5 cm

3 Toknot, 2002, polyester cord, 100 metre cord

4 Out of the Dark, 2001/2002, gold, fabric, bone black pigment, lamp black pigment and oil paint, 3.8 x 3.6 x 4 x 4.8 cm

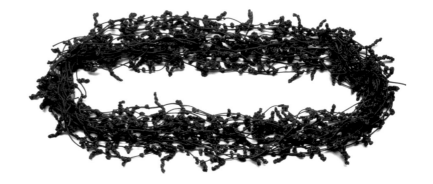

Solange Azagury-Partridge
Lara Bohinc
Erickson Beamon
Elizabeth Galton
Shaun Leane
Daisuke Sakaguchi
Wouters & Hendrix

FASHION FORWARD

Solange Azagury-Partridge

Iconoclasm at its finest, Solange Azagury-Partridge's irreverent designs are as unconventionally glamourous as her own career history. In 1987, after several years working in top London jewellers, Solange created her first piece — her own engagement ring — an uncut diamond in a simple gold band. Though her first creation stemmed from her inability to find a ready-made ring, her subsequent designs were eclectically inspired. "Absolutely anything inspires me", declares Solange, as her playful collections demonstrate. Without any formal training, Solange works from a single principle — her desire to subvert expectations and concoct the unexpected.

In Crop Circle Earrings, 2004, extraterrestrial meets Art Deco where black gold and green diamonds' symmetries conspire, yet her burlesque aesthetic shines even brighter in Vices and Virtues Ring, 2002, in which the wearer's moral decorum is made as prominent as bling itself. Her Fringe Ring, 1998, brings 18 ct gold to the costume (and hairstyle) of 1980s metal, and her Days of the Week Ring, 2002, honours literally the banality of every day. By merging the material and technique of fine jewellery with the robust aesthetics of the popular and the rebellious, Solange's jewellery is both ironic and seductive — and, perhaps not unexpectedly, avant-garde.

1 The Big Bang, 2003, 18 ct white gold and diamond

2 Days of the Week Ring, 2002, 18 ct red gold, ruby, diamonds, and enamel

3 The Catherine Wheel Ring, 2005, 18 ct black gold and multicolored stones, 2.2 cm diameter

4 The Eye Ring, 1998, 18 ct gold with rubies and onyx, 1.8 x 2.2 cm

5 Fringe Ring, 1998, 18 ct white gold, 1.5 cm square

6 Vices and Virtues Ring, 2002, 18 ct yellow gold and diamond, 2.2 x 1.5 cm

Lara Bohinc

Trained in industrial design before completing her MA in jewellery at the Royal College of Art, London, Lara Bohinc's clean and minimalist designs are clearly influenced by her architectural beginnings. Plastic, leather, wood, and metal provide a platform for her often geometric constructions, and her work tends toward clean, optical lines remniscent of 1960s prints. With colours kept bold and basic, her jewellery designs maintain the essential without becoming too bare. By applying innovative techniques such as laser-cutting and photo-etching to create her work, Bohinc follows her aesthetic upbringing and her taste for precision by bringing these technical methods to fine jewellery production.

In Curb Chain Necklace, 2004, a chunky black gold-plated brass chain is surprisingly juxtaposed with a cluster of shiny silver beads for a look that is equally strong and glamourous. Long Drop Earrings, 2004, are strikingly modern and mature in their refined symmetry, whilst Peacock Choker, 2004, (modelled by the designer herself) offers a more casual and bohemian alternative to the polished metals and precious stones of her other collections. Bohinc's Oval Box Bag, 2004, demonstrates her abilities beyond jewellery design, and Butterfly Disc Necklace, 2004, further exemplifies her signature style — sharp, clean, and feminine.

1	2	3

1 Curb Chain Necklace, 2004, black gold-plated brass with silver 925 hallmarked beads, 32 x 19 cm

2 Butterfly Disc Necklace, 2004, black-plated gold with synthetic diamonds, 20 x 28 cm

3 Peacock Choker, 2003, laser-cut leather, 10 x 24 cm

photography:
Daniel Swallow

Erickson Beamon

With a flair for fashion that fuels their creative instincts, designers Vicki Bea Sarge and Karen Erickson arrived in New York in 1982 and quickly established their shop and their reputation amid the scenesters of Manhattan's Upper East Side. Quickly building their accessory collection, Erickson Beamon acquired a clientele as vast and diverse as their designs. With just over 20 years of success, their signature style maintains its baroque inspiration – think 1980s costume jewellery meets belle époque – yet their contemporary collections draw their influences from various cultures and eras –from 'Josephine Baker', to 'Funk-a-delic', to 'Navajo'. Their ever-glamourous style is driven and maintained not only by their clientele but by their consistent collaboration with top designers' runway shows.

Their original designs evoke a particular vintage glamour that is as flirtatious as it is dramatic. The headdress, 2005, designed for Swarovski, exemplifies their commitment to the delicate artistry that goes into the production of such an intricate and elegant piece. The belt buckle choker, combining leather with silver and crystal embellishments, reveals their ability to bring their signature style to new and reinvented forms. In another neckpiece, the variety of elements and lavish layers, all delicately draped to create a look of casual bohemian-glam, demonstrates the versatility in their adherence to glamour.

1 Swarovski crystal headdress, 2005, modelled by Erin O'Connor, Jenny Packham Autumn/Winter 2005 fashion show

2 Necklace from Hotrocks collection, Autumn/Winter 2004, leather and crystal

3 Necklace from Josephine Baker collection, Autumn/Winter 2004, crystal, pearl and horn

Elizabeth Galton

Dispensing with the usual catches, clasps and chains, Elizabeth Galton's florid and theatrical pieces of sculptural proportion are more metallic extensions of the body than demure ornaments. Her jewellery is hyperbolic couture; it commands of its viewer absolute attention while it demands of its wearer an exercise in adventurous adornment. Described by Mayfair Life as "the most wearably eccentric concoctions to have been spied on the style scene for some time", Galton's pieces seem to stray into a field of overblown ornamentation, but nonetheless maintain their prescribed relationship to the human form, often grasping on to areas of the body that have been forgotten by most jewellery designers.

Inspired by the life cycle of flowers, particularly the form of the orchid, Galton denies her work the usual prosaic floral patterns and aspires to embody the ephemeral and the eternal through the shock of the massive and monumental. "They are dying as they bloom", she insists, but there is little doubt that her spectacularly styled jewels are soon to wilt.

1 King Dragon Waistpiece, 2000, silver and aluminum, photography: Holly Jolliffe, model: Emie Elg

2 Orchid Gem for Swarovski Runway Rocks, 2004, rhodium-plated silver with Swarovski crystal, 33 x 22 cm wide, photography: Tim Griffiths courtesy Swarovski, London

3 Orchid Gem for Swarovski Runway Rocks, 2004, rhodium-plated silver with Swarovski crystal, 33 x 22 cm wide photography: Doug Rosa

Shaun Leane

Shaun Leane is a London-based jeweller who is aware of and engages with what has been fashionable about the city since the early 1990s. He began to establish his career through working with the enfant-terrible and general fashion bad-boy Alexander McQueen on his second runway show, Highland Rape, in 1992. The two have maintained a fruitful working relationship ever since. Leane's style, in McQueen's words, combines "structure with finesse", a description which seems to only modestly capture Leane's ability to juxtapose seemingly sadistic piercing movements alongside delicate touches of texture. His work has evolved with the times; Leane has moved beyond the Gothic aesthetic that launched his career (he titled his 1997 solo exhibition Violently Elegant). His recent earrings evoke the frantic display of parrots and some playful yet disturbing copper earpieces are reminiscent of sculptural discs, giving the impression of an encounter with a primitive culture from outer space. Pushing the boundaries of catwalk fashion jewellery, his pieces have varied widely in dimensions — from the small anklet to the full-scale encrusted body-sculpture — but they always remain in the domain of the sensual, moulding together elements of the fleshly and the metallic in a frightening futurism that has helped define the London fashion experiment.

1 Poison Ring, Diamond collection 2005, 18 ct white gold and rubies

2 Parrot Fan Feather Earrings, 2003, parrot feathers, Shaun Leane for Alexander McQueen Irere show Spring/Summer 2003

3 Interlocking ring set, 2004, 18 ct white gold and diamonds

4 Sabre Bangle, 2003, ivory resin and ruby and silver cap

5 The Full Tusk Bracelet, Signature collection 2000, silver

Daisuke Sakaguchi

Young designer Daisuke Sakaguchi represents the spirit and style of the street in his hip-hop and urban-inspired rings, bracelets, and belt buckle designs. Stemming from his experience in graffiti art, Sakaguchi models his jewellery pieces after the style of tags and aspires to create art that can be worn. "I've always been inspired by fashion", he says, but fashion as an expression of personal style rather than a reflection of high street trends. "I feel strongly about the concept of identity", he says, and sees the streets as opportunity for "public art exhibition". Sakaguchi has explored other areas of fashion design, but making three-dimensional objects has proved more interesting to him than working with fabric, leading to his focus on jewellery and metalwork.

While his intentions are genuine, Sakaguchi is not without humour and irony, reflecting the loudness of urban and street culture in the oversized gaud he creates. The almost over-the-top double finger Fidgit split ring, 2003, was the outcome of a tattoo turned logo that Sakaguchi designed for DJ Fidgit, with the ring design being split to remain practical for heavy DJ use. The angles and distortions of his belt buckle and bracelet designs also demonstrate his instinctive street style and his attraction to "the repeated strokes of expressive lines in an aim to create visually stimulating images".

1 Double finger Fidgit split ring, Nocturnal bracelet, True Agenda belt buckle, all 2003, hallmarked 925 sterling silver, photography: Richard Grassie, model: Ruth Crilly, styling: Jamie Brickwood, make-up: Dani Guinsberg, hair: Dino@1

2 Double finger Fidgit split ring, 2003, hallmarked 925 sterling silver, photography: Holly Jolliffe

Wouters & Hendrix

The Belgian duo Wouters & Hendrix (first names Katrin and Karen respectively) met whilst studying at the Royal Academy of Fine Arts in Antwerp, graduating in the misty past of 1984. Since that time they have steadily released collection after collection (always titled with a twist, from their Healing Jewellery to the Carnival of Emotions), building up a professional client base, ranging from hip-hop starlet Kelis to the comedian Lenny Henry. They also have an impressive history of collaborations with prestigious fashion designers under their belt – from fellow Belgian avant-gardist Ann Demeulemeester to the more bo-ho Paul & Joe. In 2001, after almost 20 years in the business, they opened their own flagship store in Antwerp, permanently establishing their presence on the high street as well as on catwalk collections.

Their jewellery combines the eclectic (and at times eccentrically ad hoc) with an attentive eye for detailed quality. This manifests itself in interesting combinations of silverwork with large stones and organic material (such as dickhorn and coral), with their designs ranging from the effortlessly subtle to the playfully childish. Using a palette of 'bare' colours – black, grey and iridescent white, with the occasional shock of green and electric blue – a recent collection draws on Chinese mythology in the form of Oriental-inspired hand-finished lace jewellery and the occasional symbolically imprinted jade encrusted necklace. Combining an escapism with sumptuous design their jewellery is the choice of those with a need for quirky elegance.

1	2	
3	4	5

1 Katrin Wouters and Karin Hendrix

2 Multi-strand copper coloured necklace, Spring/Summer 2005, anodised aluminium, 55 cm, photography: Ren Keller

3 Left to right: Jadeit pastille in sterling silver setting; Lace inspired sterling silver ring; Solid sterling silver ring with square mother of pearl; Shiny oval solid sterling silver ring, Autumn/Winter 2004, photography: Ren Keller

4 Left to right: Horn earrings, 4.5 cm; Multi-strand solid silver sautoir, 65 cm; Snakeskin cuff with solid silver clasp, 15.5-17.5 cm; Chocolate brown calf leather cuff with solid silver clasp, 15.5-17.5 cm; Solid sterling silver ring with chain pattern, Autumn/Winter 2004, photography: Ren Keller

5 Knitted sterling silver christening gown, 70 cm high, Spring/Summer 2002, photography: Ren Keller

Anna Osmer Andersen
Kristina Apostolou
Tomasz Donocik
Arline Fisch
Danielle Gordon
Maria Hanson
Adele Kime
Daniela Schwartz
Vannetta Seecharran
Sissi Westerberg
Christoph Zellweger

TACTILE SCULPTURE

|1|2|
|3|4|

1 Twisted Necklace, 2004, vintage fabrics and polyester filling

2 Belt Pom-Pom, 2001, vintage fabrics

3 Pearl Necklace, 2004, vintage fabrics and polyester filling

4 Chain Necklace, 2004, vintage fabrics and polyester filling

model: Anna Ruperg

Anna Osmer Andersen

Anna Osmer Andersen is known for her oversized textile-based jewellery that makes the wearer appear like a child dressing up in her mother's necklaces. This is most striking when the work represents a traditional piece of jewellery as in Pearl Necklace, 2004. The works are made from fabrics pieced together in patchwork constructions, the softness of the material allowing the large-scale items to be comfortably worn. For Chain Necklace, 2004, another work in this collection, Andersen uses fabric to replace and mimic the conventionally metal links of chain necklace. While all of the pieces in the series are larger than life and have the potential to weigh the wearer down, or in the case of Chain Necklace, can appear as a burden or bind, the soft padded tactile qualities of the works make them embraceable.

Andersen's earlier series of Pom-Pom belts and necklaces, 2001, arose out of collecting patterned vintage material. The colourful swatches are sewn together to form pom-poms that resemble carnations. By relishing the rough fraying edges of the antique materials, these works make evident Andersen's appreciation for the formal qualities of fabric.

"The use of traditional chains is the main theme, linking repeated shapes, which allows for flexibility of movement and variation in scale."

Kristina Apostolou

Kristina Apostolou's Ylyr... signature collection consists of textile-based necklaces and bracelets that blur the boundary between clothing, jewellery and wearable art. Capitalising on the intrinsic qualities of the natural fibre, sinamay, Apostolou's works maintain the fluid folding movement of fabric whilst incorporating the precious metals of traditional jewellery.

Sinamay, a material often used in millinery, forms the basis for each piece, encircling the neck or wrist in elaborate folds and bold curves. The material appears free flowing and malleable, but the works hold their carefully manipulated shape, elegantly encasing the body. For her Ylyr... signature Neckpieces, 2004, Apostolou lines the fabric's edge with gold-plated metal giving the otherwise chaotic ensemble a clarifying linear accent. The gold trim on the black sinamai of her Ylyr... signature Handpiece, 2004 is echoed by a ring of gold that curves in the opposite direction of the fabric and pierces the openings of the porous material. The transparency of the material simultaneously covers and reveals the skin, while the curvilinear forms emphasise the contours of the body.

"Drawing inspiration from a variety of sources, such as nature, history and fashion my vision was to create a collection of work that adorns and celebrates the sumptuousness of the female body."

1 Ylyr... signature Neckpiece, 2004, sinamay, black enamel, gold-plated metal ribbon and gold-plated chain

2 Ylyr... signature Handpiece, 2004, sinamay, black enamel, gold-plated metal ribbon and gold-plated chain

3 Ylyr... signature Neckpiece, 2004, sinamay, ivory enamel, gold-plated metal ribbon and gold-plated chain

4 Ylyr... signature Neckpiece and Handpiece, 2004, sinamay, ivory enamel, gold-plated metal ribbon and gold-plated chain

photographer:
Benjamin Kaufmann

model: Gabriella Rabelo at ICM models

hair/make-up:
Dina at ERAmanagement

1 Leather Bracelet, 2004, brown leather cow skin, "pony skin", citrine set into silver screws, 16 cm diameter

2 Scarf with 18 Leather Balls, detail, 2004, 18 stretched hollow leather balls all connected at the top, leather, silver rim, tourmaline and citrine set into silver screws, each ball 5 cm diameter

3 Enslavement Bracelet, 2004, silver arm bracelet gold-plated, with green leather and tourmaline/ citrine screws, attached with silver chain to green hollow leather ball, leather ball 20 cm diameter and bracelet 15 cm diameter

4 Leather Wraparound, 2004, "pony skin", citrine set into silver screws, 14 cm diameter

5 In Between Finger Ring, 2004, silver and manmade citrine, 3.5 cm diameter

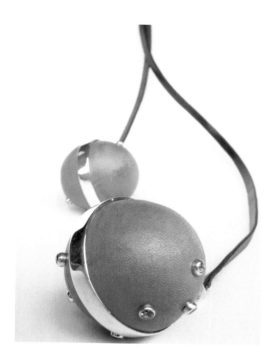

Tomasz Donocik

Working with leather, precious metals and gemstones, Tomasz Donocik designs jewellery to be worn primarily by men. These works appear to be influenced by the trappings of S&M and the glamour of costume jewellery, with their formal qualities combining the leather of bondage gear with the glitter of oversized gemstones. Donocik speaks of his jewellery as "armour that both protects and constricts", but it is also playful, lightweight and wearable.

Enslavement Bracelet, 2004, is a gold-plated silver arm bracelet which looks like a miniature medieval ball and chain. Because of this association and the scale of the ball, it looks heavy, however, it is actually made from lightweight, hollowed-out leather. Donocik uses this visual symbolism to "illustrate our dependence and subsequent enslavement of and by ourselves" and to "heighten the wearer's awareness of themselves". He transforms the iconography of restriction into a playful object of decoration and excess. His piece entitled Scarf with 18 Leather Balls, 2004, consists of several bright orange leather globes each encircled by a band of silver and studded with orange manmade citrine stones. With this work, and others, Donocik develops his visual vocabulary, pulling it further away from the original association of imprisonment by adding colour and jewels.

Arline Fisch

Working mainly with silver and gold, Arline Fisch creates intricate interlaced patterns resulting in jewellery that is subtle yet ornate. Fisch pioneered the technique of using precious and non-precious metals in the same way that fabrics are traditionally used, with her book, Textile Techniques in Metal, 1975, having for decades taught and influenced many young artists and jewellers, and continues to do so. She makes large-scale jewellery and body ornaments by braiding, knitting, crocheting and weaving metals into structures that relate to textiles, transforming cold, stiff metals into soft, pliable cloth like structures that are able to fit comfortably on the human body.

Fisch's pieces often resemble clothing worn in ancient cultures; metal-lace Egyptian-inspired collars as well as necklaces and arm pieces made from crocheted metal fibres, which echo a knight's chain-mail armour. Her designs range from more traditional beaded necklaces as in Seven Crochet Beads, 2003, to the playful bright red ruffles of Bracelet and Glove Arm Ornament, 1999.

"The use of textile structures such as weaving and braiding enable me to produce pliable planes which conform readily to the human form, and which have a softness and warmth not always possible in metals."

1 Bracelet and Glove Arm Ornament, 1999, coated copper, fine silver, machine and hand knit, photography: William Gullette, collection of the Smithsonian American Art Museum, Washington, DC

2 Lacy Net, 2001, fine silver, coated copper wire (crocheted) and sterling silver wire ovals (forged), 48 cm outer diameter, 20 cm band

3 Seven Crochet Beads, 2003, fine silver and coated copper wire (crocheted), sterling 'beads' in between, pearls inside crochet beads, 30 cm diameter, individual beads 7.5 cm diameter

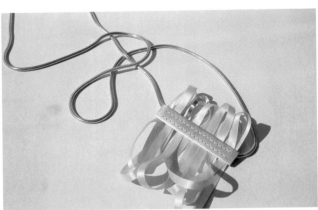

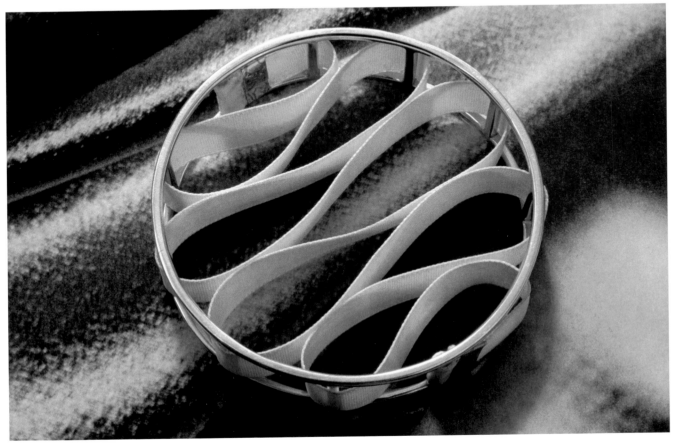

Danielle Gordon

Danielle Gordon's jewellery, made exclusively from silver and ribbon, is both original and wearable. Her unique collection of rings, brooches, bracelets and necklaces take inspiration from modern architecture and contemporary fashion design. These works also make evident Gordon's thorough investigation of the various ways in which these two materials, with their opposing qualities of lightness and weight, malleability and strength, can be elegantly integrated to support one another.

In all of her pieces the solid silver provides a framework that determines the way in which the ribbon folds and takes on shape. In works such as Window Pendant and Circular Ribbon Bangle, 2004, the ribbon loops in elegant curves through openings in the silver structure, whilst in Aperture Bangle, 2004, the ribbon has been carefully sewn through tiny holes in the surrounding metal band. The shape of all of these pieces is altered once again when they are worn. When Aperture is worn, the hand pushes through the small opening, the ribbon's final 'aperture' controlled by the size of the wearer's wrist.

"My work has taken inspiration from the architect Santiago Calatrava and fashion designer John Galliano. By fusing two contrasting materials, ribbon and silver, I have produced a range of contemporary, fashionable jewellery which is intriguing to view and comfortable to wear."

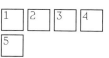

1 Long Brooch, 2004, silver, satin ribbon, thread and steel pin, 12 x 5 x 0.5 cm

2 Ribbon Neckpiece with Gold Detail, 2004, 18 ct gold, silver, satin ribbon and thread, 8 x 10 x 0.5 cm

3 Window Pendant, 2004, silver and satin ribbon, 2.5 x 2.5 x 0.7 cm

4 Aperture Bangle, 2004, silver, satin ribbon and thread, 7 cm diameter

5 Circular Ribbon Bangle, 2004, silver and satin ribbon, 7 cm diameter

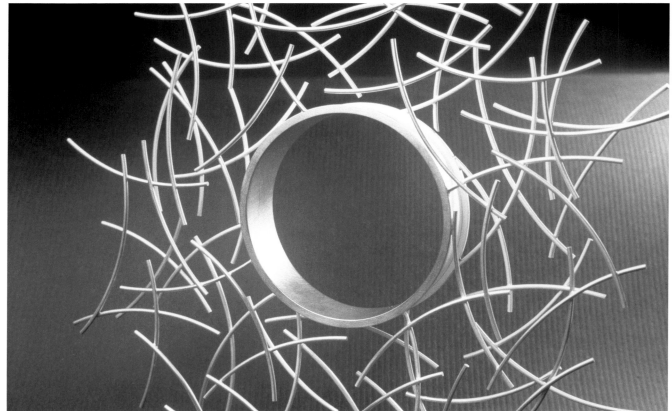

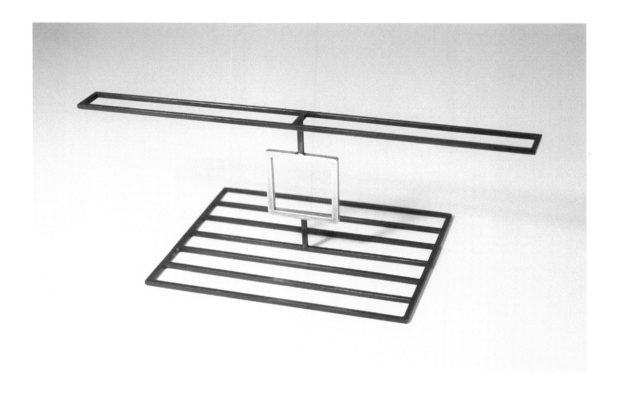

Maria Hanson

Maria Hanson's work is characterised by a fascination with materials and form. Using the traditional materials and methods of the jeweller and silversmith, she explores concerns that have a closer relationship to those of a sculptor. Hanson is as concerned with how her works function in space as freestanding objects as she is with how they relate to the body when worn.

Her pieces Enclosure no. 5, 2000, and Order and Chaos, 1998, are self-supporting objects to which the wearer's body must conform. Both pieces have balanced symmetrical compositions but deal with contrasting formal elements, and are visual responses to the terms that make up their respective titles. Enclosure is worn as a ring, the finger placed through the square opening at the structure's centre, the linear metal forms jutting out below and above the hand and consequently controlling the hand's movement and curtailing its ability to touch in a conventional way. Similarly, with Order and Chaos, the bulkiness of the piece due to its lengthy diameter makes it cumbersome to wear.

"This new collection of work is a combination of jewellery, objects and vessels. The visual language used investigates form, structure and balance and combines precious metal with non-precious elements."

1 Interlock no. 1, 2004, oxidised silver, gold leaf and black ribbon, length 100 cm, gold disk 10 cm, bead 6 x 4 cm

2 Interlock no. 2, 2004, silver, gold leaf and blue ribbon, length 90 cm, round form 6 cm, bead 6 x 4 cm

3 Enclosure no. 5, 2000, steel and white metal, 10 x 6 x 6 cm

4 Order and Chaos, 1998, silver, 20 x 20 x 2 cm

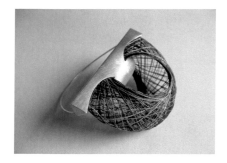

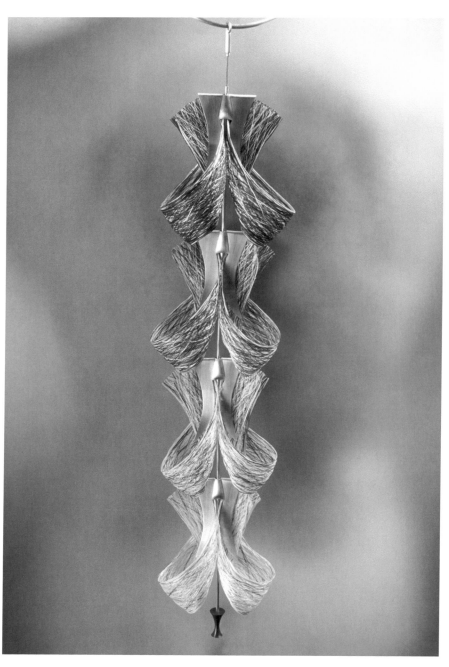

1 Loop Brooch, 2004, white
precious metal and textile
fibre, 6 x 4 x 2.5 cm

2 Free Flow Backpiece, 2002,
white precious metal, textile
fibre and anodised aluminum,
61 x 8.15 x 4 cm,
photography: Tas Kyprianou

3 Pitcher Brooch, 2003,
white and yellow precious
metal and textile fibre,
7 x 5 x 4 cm,
photography: Steve Yates

4 Pod Neckpiece, 2004, white
precious metal and textile
fibre, 7 x 4 x 3 cm

5 Self Seed Earrings, 2004,
yellow precious metal and
textile fibre, 6 x 2 x 2 cm

Adele Kime

"My work is inspired by nature's way of encasing and protecting.
I wish to create sensuous forms which when worn or viewed will
give pleasure and invite intrigue or speculation around their concept
and construction."

Adele Kime's work is centred on the intricate weaving of coloured
thread fibres held together by solid silver. Kime has spent some
years perfecting this method of construction, working intuitively with
the textile fibre to come up with the shape of each piece. Her
structures are reminiscent of birds' nests in that the delicacy of the
weaving is in contradiction to the strength of the actual construction,
commenting that "when handled it is unexpected to find the delicate
structures hard to touch".

Kime perceives her work as both sculpture and jewellery, saying
"whether a piece of my work is seen as jewellery, sculpture or both
is decided upon by the viewer or wearer". Free Flow, 2004 is a back
piece which appears as a cascade of repeated entwined ultramarine
blue and silver mesh, echoing the spine that it hangs over. Kime
also makes more conventionally sized pieces such as Loop Earrings
and Loop Brooch, both 2004, in which the transparency of the mesh
allows the skin or clothing beneath to integrate and complement the
subtle colours of the fibres.

1 Through the Skin... Inside
Out Choker, 2003, sterling
silver, green wool, organic
lens 'Grey 2' and latex

2 From the Bones... Inside
Out Choker, 2002, sterling
silver, polyethylene, gold
latex, turquoise angora and
Swarovski crystals

3 Through the Skin... Inside
Out Ring, 2003, sanded,
sulfurated sterling silver
and wool

4 Through the Skin... Inside
Out Bracelet, 2003, sterling
silver, grey wool, organic
lens 'Grey 3' and latex

photography: Florencia Rosner

models: Maria Alleman and
Leonora Balcarce

Daniela Schwartz

Daniela Schwartz constructs her jewellery taking advantage of the wide range of materials available in the contemporary industrial world, incorporating latex and polyethylene with glass, precious metals and wool. The expertise and detail with which she combines natural handmade materials with industrially produced synthetics, as well as textile fibres with more traditional jewellery materials such as silver and crystals, is what makes her work unique.

In terms of content, Schwartz's personal practice as a dancer has fuelled her fascination with the workings of the body, and informs her jewellery design. She assembles her contrasting materials together to refer to parts of the body; coloured latex tubing is evocative of the circulatory system, and chunky knitted wool becomes a second skin for the wearer. The impetus behind her work is to "open up the body and bring what is hidden inside out into everyday life".

Her piece From the Skin... Inside Out Choker, 2002, made from carefully knitted wool that hugs the skin like a snug winter sweater, crosses the boundary between textiles and jewellery. When worn, the piece constricts the neck whilst allowing the rest of the body freedom to move around, calling the wearer's attention to this specific body part. Her Through the Skin... Inside Out Rings, 2003, demonstrate her attention to detail; tiny angora fibres line the circular cavities of the sterling sliver structure, again incorporating textiles with conventional jewellery elements.

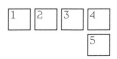

1 Bangle, 2000, silver and
red ribbons, 9 cm diameter,
ribbon length 4 cm

2 Sleeve, 2003, blue satin
fabric, red ribbon and
red thread

3 Bangle, 2002, silver and
black ribbons, 9 cm diameter,
ribbon length 7 cm

4 Cuff, 1998, silver and red
velvet, silver: height 9.5 cm

5 Sleeve, 2003, green satin
fabric and gold thread

photographer: Grant Hancock
model: Katrina Webber

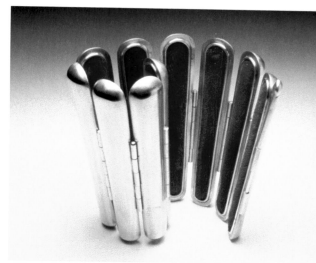

Vannetta Seecharran

Vannetta Seecharran's jewellery appeals to the eye as well as to the touch by combining tactile textiles such as velvet and ribbon with the precious metal silver. They are designed in such a way so that the silver provides the framework by which the soft materials are held to the skin as in Cuff, 1998, in which red velvet is encased in individual silver test tube shaped structures that are linked together with hinges. This aspect of the piece reflects Seecharran's intention "to create a dialogue between two materials so that neither is dominant but instead can work harmoniously".

Seecharran's Sleeves, 2003, constructed primarily from fabric and coloured thread, partly cover and protrude from the body in a way more similar to evening wear than to traditional jewellery, crossing the boundary between fashion and jewellery in their unique use of sweeping textiles. Billowing layered satin flows from the extremities of the body rather than from the bodice. The Sleeves fit tightly along the entire arm stretching out and expanding into larger shapes that hang own from the wrist and flow to the ground. They were inspired by the ocean, taking on its green and blue colour, as well as its ebb and flow in terms of curving organic shapes.

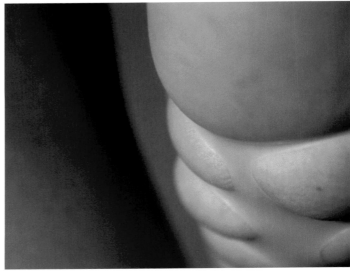

Sissi Westerberg

Sissi Westerberg has a dynamic and playful approach to jewellery design, using a myriad of materials and processes. Behind the Curtains, 2000, takes the shape of a pair of spectacles but are made from silver-plated brass. She sawed through the metal to create the delicate pattern copied from a piece of lace purchased in Jerusalem. Even though the surface of the 'glasses' is porous, due to the pattern, the wearer's gaze would be severely restricted by them. Flesh, 2002, is a bracelet/armband that when worn changes the surface and shape of one's skin, pulling it tighter and allowing it to bulge out forming a fleshy pattern. These two very different works are similar in the way that the pattern of holes in both allow the wearer, their skin and gaze respectively, to pass through the jewellery itself, and in this way serves to highlight the boundaries of the body.

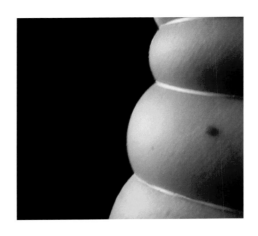

Her series of brooches entitled Connections II, 2002, are small loose "buds of flesh", "the body's inlets and outlets", as she puts it, made from red and pink silicon rubber. They look as if they are casts of the interior of belly buttons, an interior cavity made into something solid. The playfulness of these pieces is also evident in her cartoony brooch Something Inside, 2004, which is to be worn just outside of a breast pocket so that it looks as if the drips of red silicone are seeping out from inside it.

1 Something Inside, 2004, silicone, 10 cm

2 Flesh, 2002, latex, still from video, photography: Carl Schonebohm

3 Connections II, 2002, silicone, 3 x 3 x 2 cm

4 Flesh, 2002, rubber band, still from video, photography: Carl Schonebohm

5 Behind the Curtains, 2000, silver-plated brass, 15 x 15 x 6 cm

6 Let Go I, 2002, pearls and silicone, 20 x 20 cm

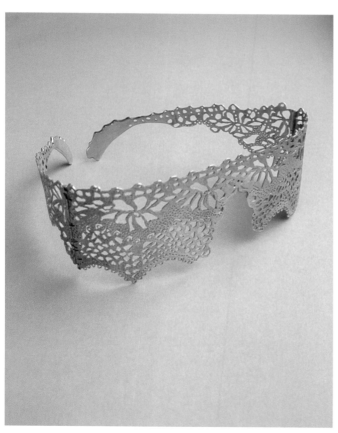

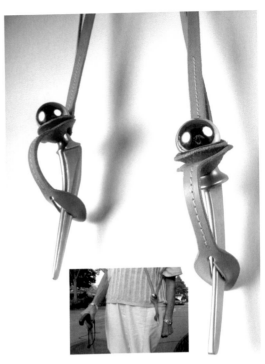

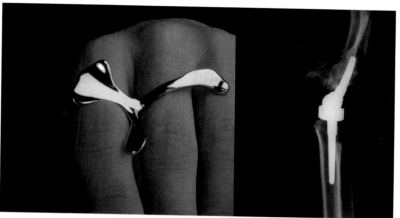

Christoph Zellweger

Christoph Zellweger's jewellery questions contemporary notions of the body and the role that adornment plays in terms of its function and aesthetic. Much of his work takes its influence from the ways in which we can now augment the body with prosthetic parts and implants. His pieces force us to question whether we value the body as whole as opposed to the sum of its parts.

Some of the steel pendants in his series entitled Foreign Bodies, such as hip piece — neck piece, 2002, incorporates a second-hand prosthesis, while others, namely the Fluids, 2002, are all manufactured by himself in cast medical steel, a hi-tec material chosen by Zellweger because of its preciousness and the connections to the body. The shiny pendants are supported by long harness-like leather straps that can be adapted freely to one's anatomy. The soft and liquid-looking forms of the Fluids contrast strongly with the sharp almost violent looking devices of hip piece — neck piece. With Foreign Bodies, Zellweger also refers to the traditional, sentimental function of jewellery. Foreign Body pendants can be worn as a way of remembering the person whose body performance had once been improved by the insertion of a perfectly made, highly valuable precious metal implant. The symbiosis of body and object is not ever-lasting, whilst the highly polished steel is.

"Now we can commodify the body. It can be aestheticised beyond body adornment of past cultures; actually, the body becomes the adornment."

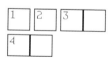

1 Fluids, 2002, cast medical steel (ceramic shell casting) and leather, fluids 4-6 cm, length of leather 70 cm

2 hip piece — neck piece, 2002, second hand medical steel prosthesis and leather, overall length of leather 80 cm, prosthesis 17 x 5 x 5 cm

3 Commodity no. 6, 1998, chrome-plated 18 ct gold, hallmarked, steel pin, 6 x 4 x 2.5 cm

4 Body Pieces, 1996-1997, expanded polystyrene, chrome-plated silver, silicone tubing, 7-14 cm

Elizabeth Bone
Gill Forsbrook
Laura Gates
Marina Molinelli Wells
Kamilla Ruberg

NEW GEOMETRIES

Elizabeth Bone

Working primarily in precious metals, Elizabeth Bone's designs exhibit a distinctly modernist balance and symmetry, whilst also conjuring up a sense of origin and evolution through her use of elemental forms. In her order and precision she refers visually to a mechanical production, although each of her constructions are made through manual processes — sawing, filing, shaping and coaxing. Bone's aesthetic is simple, with themes and order emerging in the process itself — with their occurrence being as important to her as the final product.

Her pendulum-like designs for necklaces and pendants evoke both Art Deco and natural sensibilities in the alternating rhythms of silver and gold, sun and moon. The lunar influence appears in Moon Necklaces, 2002, where cool and cleanly cut disks freely dangle alongside stacked orbs that swell at the base. In Growth Ring Brooch, 2000, the thin ring form evolves into an elegantly expanding brooch. Her stacking rings, 1999, which can be worn in sets of three, have varying geometric cutouts which form different shapes depending on the combination worn, continuing Bone's experimentation with abstraction.

"Material and process guided by order, balance, and a modernist influence form the basis for my work."

1	2
3	4

1 Growth Ring Brooch, 2000,
silver, 18 ct gold-plate, 8 cm

2 Moon Necklaces, 2002,
silver, 100-104 cm long

3 Separate rings to be worn
together in groups of three,
1999, silver, 4 cm diameter

4 Moon Ring, 2001, silver,
4-7 cm

photography: Joël Degen

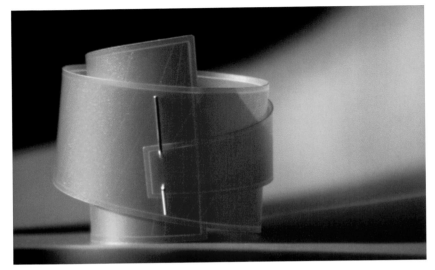

Gill Forsbrook

Polypropylene, polycarbonate, acrylic, and PVC — the names of plastics used in Gill Forsbrook's jewellery demand a flexibility of the tongue that equals that of the materials themselves. In fact, this malleability is a great deal of what appeals to Forsbrook. By exploring these different types of plastics, she develops designs for a range of jewellery pieces — bangles, earrings and pendants — and further exploits qualities of the materials beyond mere plasticity. While she denies preference for a particular medium, she admits an affinity for glass works, with her products' layers and contrasts evidence of her interest in variations in colour, translucency, and transparency. Forsbrook also prefers not to choose any particular artist who has influenced her work, but recalls admiring as a student the new Dutch jewellery designers of the late 1970s such as Emmy van Leersum.

Forsbrook's pendants, which also use aluminum, rubber, and silver, are simple but funky. Spiralling and overlapping layers in a bangle or undulating bands within a bounded circle, Forsbrook is not afraid to experiment freely with shapes. The zigzag in the bangle appears to deny its wearability, but when worn, the waves expand and contract to the shape of one's arm, a design that demonstrates Forsbrook's equally impressive flexibility in conception.

1 Bangle, 2001,
polypropylene, polycarbonate
and silver, 9 x 9 cm

2 Pendants, 2003,
polypropylene, acrylic, PVC,
aluminium, rubber and silver,
largest diameter: 3.5 cm

3 Bangle, 2004,
polypropylene, polycarbonate
and silver, 14.5 x 13 x 3 cm

4 Bangles, 2002,
polypropylene, PVC,
aluminium and silver,
4.5 x 7 cm

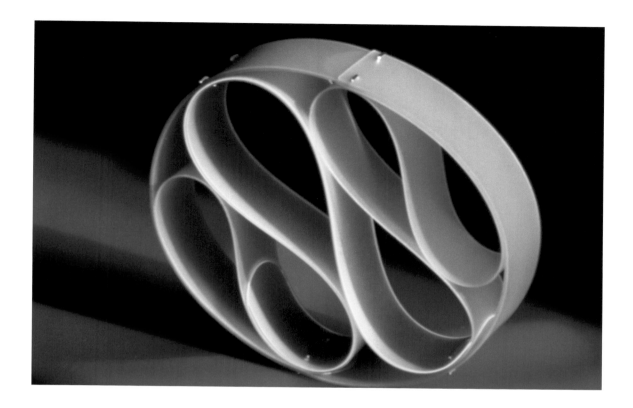

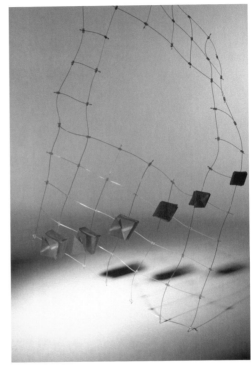

Laura Gates

Laura Gates' jewellery designs are distinguished not only by their use of bright colour, but by their unusual materials and shapes. Gates typically begins her designs with sheet nylon that she has cut, scored, and hand-dyed. From this delicately coloured material, she creates miniature boxes that she incorporates into her designs in a variety of ways. In her Box-Grid Jewellery, 2000, she suspends the boxes in an ethereal grid of woven nylon filament, and in the Box-Hoop range, also 2000, she aligns the boxes and combines them with gold leaf to create intricate and lightweight bangles and neckpieces.

Gates recognises that nylon is uncommon in jewellery design and embraces the way its qualities can contribute to the "colourful, decorative world we live in". In her Spira-line jewellery, 2002, she twists different filaments to create curiously subtle chains of colour. In fact, it's the ability of her pieces to evoke curiosity in the viewer that drives Gates' design, combining the delicate geometric folding of origami shapes with the malleable texture of nylon.

1 Box-Grid Bracelet, 1999, hand-dyed nylon origami

2 Box-Grid Jewellery, 2000, hand-dyed nylon origami

3 Wrist Box-Hoop, 2000, hand-dyed nylon origami

photography: P J Gates

Marina Molinelli Wells

Although simple, sharp and sleek, Marina Molinelli Wells' jewellery draws from a diverse assortment of influences. Having studied industrial design at the University of Buenos Aires, Molinelli Wells naturally translates her structural sensibilities into wearable pieces, yet her studies in glass modelling, art and dance history, special effects, and make up — in addition to five years study in contemporary jewellery — are evident in the subtle multi-dimensionality of her aesthetic framework. Posing natural and industrial elements in unlikely symmetries, she charges her pieces with a drama that appears both uninhibited and poised.

In her Pilchas collection, her use of leather and metal engages the juxtaposition of nature and industry through authentically Argentinian materials. The collection consists of 11 'mother' pieces in either sterling silver, aged gold, or sanded aged silver, which function as neckpiece bases to which the wearer is free to attach his or her own choice of leather. By varying brightness and tone in the metals, and allowing different volume, colour, and texture in the leather skins, her collection frees expression through these permutations. Molinelli Wells understands skin as the element through which we relate to our environment, and through this adornment we are similarly exposed; we are able to "reveal our internal feelings and share with others".

1 Pilchas, 2003, silver, sterling silver or gold, leather or animal skin, dimensions variable

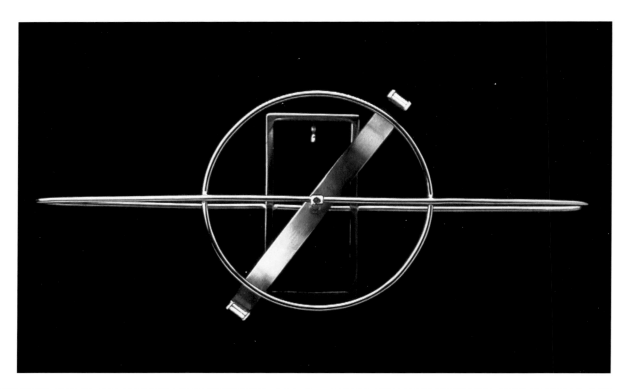

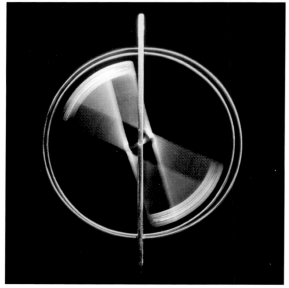

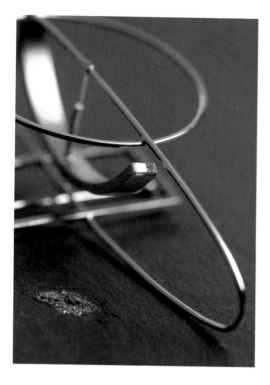
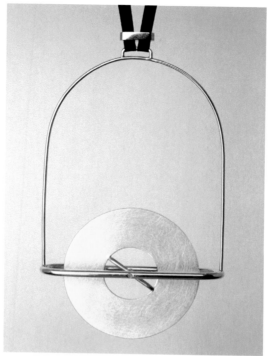

Kamilla Ruberg

The kinetic designs of Kamilla Ruberg reflect her appreciation of elegance and precision, symmetry and motion. At once decorative and revolutionary, her pieces embody a modern contradiction — the sophisticated embellishment of Art Deco jewellery meets the radical space-time exploration of constructivist sculpture. Kamilla is motivated to examine the possibilities of "balance and movement", and each of her one-off pendants and brooches draws its inspiration from her taste for "clean lines and a modern vocabulary". Yet despite the experimental element in her work, her constructions demand absolute accuracy in design and craftsmanship as well as attention to the compositional roles of weight and gravity.

The motion of her jewellery pieces is generated not only through the compositions, but is equally contingent on the wearer. "The piece becomes alive when the central part starts to spin or tremble, activated by the body's movement." While her kinetic pendants seem as though they are designed more to be seen than to be worn, this shared dynamism produces an integral connection that constantly engages the wearer and inspires greater awareness of the fluctuation of body movement. The formal emphasis on "delicate geometry" allows for a familiar aesthetic while the kinetic aspect provides for constant recreation.

1 Kinetic Brooch no. 6, 2002, 18 ct white and yellow gold, two baguette diamonds, clear polymer, 4.5 x 10.5 x 3 cm, photography: Kamilla Ruberg

2 Detail of Kinetic Brooch no. 6, 2002, photography: Holly Jolliffe

3 Kinetic Brooch no. 14, 2003, 18 ct yellow gold, six princess cut diamonds, clear polymer, 7 x 5 x 1.3 cm, photography: Kamilla Ruberg

4 Kinetic Brooch no. 6, 2002, in motion, photography: Kamilla Ruberg

5 Kinetic Pendant no. 33, 2003, 18 ct white and yellow gold, clear polymer, black ribbon, 4 x 7 x 1.2 cm, photography: Kamilla Ruberg

Vicki Ambery-Smith
Jivan Astfalck
Jo Bagshaw
Tomoko Hayashi
Alyssa Dee Krauss
Francisca Kweitel
Hannah Louise Lamb
Laura Potter
Hans Stofer

TELLING STORIES

Vicki Ambery-Smith

Vicki Ambery-Smith creates delicate and ornate small-scale jewellery and boxes inspired by real and imaginary buildings. Especially attracted to the structural clarity and minimal ornament of Romanesque and Renaissance architecture, she also uses forms reminiscent of the modernist structures of Mies van der Rohe and Frank Lloyd Wright, sometimes explicitly, as in the brooch Guggenheim Museum (NY), 1998. More recently she has become attracted to contemporary and future architecture, working on brooches based on Daniel Libeskind's bold, jarring forms, a significant move away from the classical structures with which her jewellery is associated.

As all her jewellery is designed to be worn, and worn comfortably, the three-dimensional architectural structures on which she bases her work must be adapted rather than merely replicated in miniature, with the effect of distancing them further from their original referent. In this way, attention is drawn to the form of the pieces, and their intricate detail and definition. Far more than a representation of a building, each becomes an exquisite study of shape, surface, light and space as Ambery-Smith explores the language of architecture herself.

As a result of Ambery-Smith's desire to go beyond representation, to "a more personal interpretation of the character of a building", some pieces seem to have no direct referent but are highly suggestive of certain locations or eras, appearing as tiny stage sets, on to which the viewer can project their own dramas and personal narratives of place. In this way she plays with the power of architecture to inspire fantasy, trigger memory and evoke sensations.

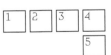

1 Penguin Pool, brooch, 1994, silver and acrylic, 4.8 x 4.1 x 1.4 cm

2 Two rings, 1985-1996, silver and yellow gold, width 2 x 3.8 cm

3 Olumuc Synagogue, ring, 2002, silver and red gold, 2.3 x 4 cm

4 Guggenheim Museum (NY), brooch, 1998, silver, 6 x 5 x 1.3 cm

5 St Paul's Cathedral Dome, brooch, 1999, silver and gold, 4.6 x 1.3 x 7.3 cm

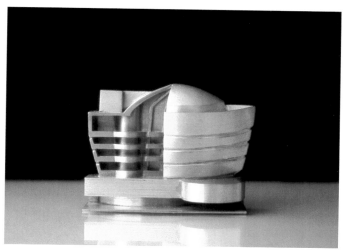

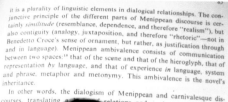

Jivan Astfalck

Drawing on historical and autobiographical material, fiction and fairy tales, Jivan Astfalck makes jewellery objects in order to tell hybrid, fantastical stories. The dynamic relationship that her "body-related objects" have with theory and literature helps to develop the narrative of a piece, however she also sees her objects as mnemonic devices, triggering memories and associations. In this way, they open up to the wearer or viewer, inviting their own contribution to be added to the existing layers of references. Bandages for Broken Hearts, 2003, for example, combines found group photographs — of schoolchildren, families, colleagues — from different eras, with a series of symbolic items made of bandage and sticking plaster. Enigmatic, yet suggestive of the wounds of history and of the trauma and healing processes that are part of our relationships with others, these objects are sites of memory and fiction, history and thought, visible traces providing connections with the invisible and imagined in a complex web of relationships.

As a result of her strong belief in the importance of narratives and fiction in our everyday lives, Astfalck's pieces have a significance reaching beyond adornment. Addressing the way in which we deal with the unknown, such as the found photographs often used, and their haunting, nameless subjects, they allow us to reflect on our "need for personalising what is alien to us, in order to understand it, even if this understanding is ultimately an illusion".

1 ... remember you, 2004, bracelet: sterling silver and vintage hand-engraved signet stones, mostly agate; brooches: vintage French memento mori, mixed media

2 Bandages for Broken Hearts, 2003, vintage photographs, bought in Prague; wound dressing, stitched with pearls and Czech/Bohemian glass cross; plaster cast of my wrist, dragonfly-wing sealed in resin, electroformed feather and garnet set silver circle; sticky plaster stitched with garnet beads; electroformed oak-leaf and twig, red thread

3 Desire in Language, 2003, book: Desire in Language by Julia Kristeva; silver set carving of a mermaid, dyed coral, possibly Chinese, burned into book

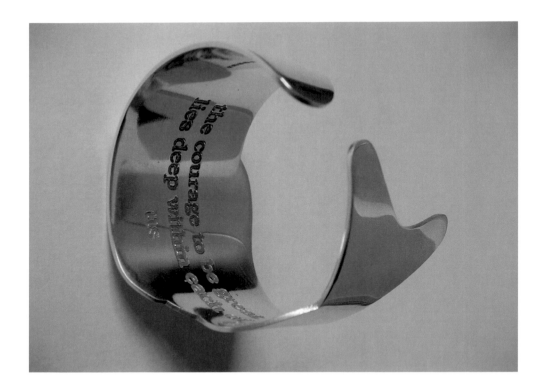

Jo Bagshaw

Jo Bagshaw works with objects and material that are normally disposable, overlooked and taken for granted, reworking them to make jewellery that rethinks conventional notions of what is precious.

The effect of a piece like Yesterday's News, 2004, lies in the fact that its individual components are not immediately recognisable. First appearing as a delicate arrangement of a repeated abstract form, only on close inspection does it become clear that it is in fact made of silver-plated chip forks engraved with newspaper print. Furthermore, this piece is a comment on the media and its tendency to relay celebrity stories in great detail whilst trivialising important news. Bagshaw asks us to review our priorities, undermining assumptions about what counts as desirable by giving the everyday and ordinary new value. However, whilst elevating the commonplace and the throwaway, Bagshaw does not rarify her original material. Eminently wearable ("comfortable, practical and fun" in her own words), even useable — as with the Fortune Fish napkin holders and key rings — her pieces give objects a "second life", as she calls it, through new use in a different context, implicating the wearer or user in this process of revaluation.

1	2
3	

1 Fortune Fish Tells Tales,
napkin ring, 2004, silver,
4.5 x 4.5 cm

2 Key Neckpiece, 2002, found
steel keys, copper wire,
36 x 34 cm

3 Yesterday's News,
neckpiece (detail), 2004,
silver-plated etched brass,
160 x 9.4 cm, photography:
Holly Jolliffe

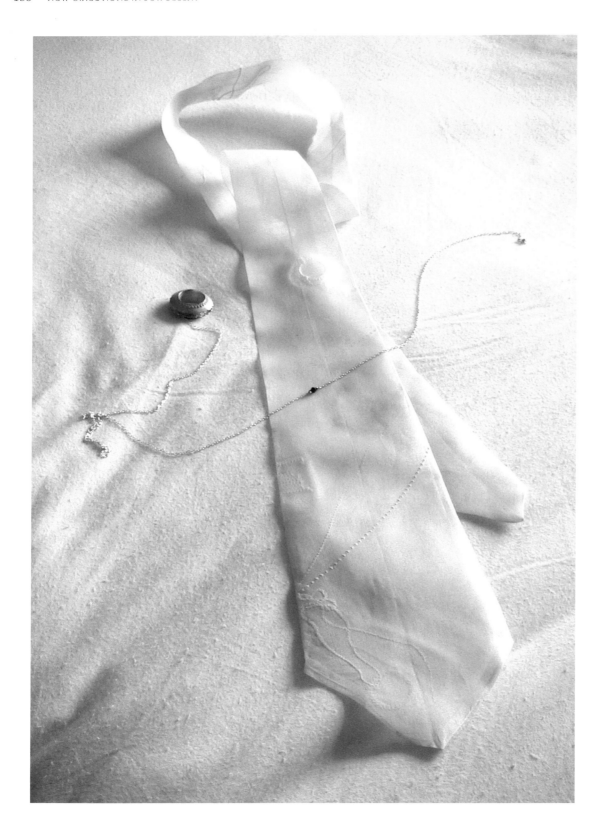

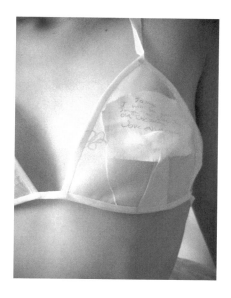
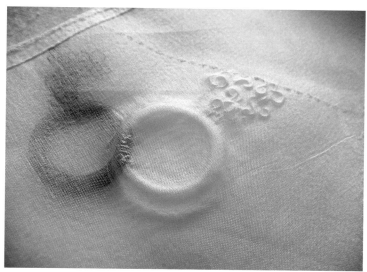

Tomoko Hayashi

With her textile-based practice, Tomoko Hayashi aims to improve communication between couples in long distance relationships. Collaborating with jeweller Marianne Anderson, she has created accessories, incorporating fabric and jewellery items, and more recently, interactive installations, in an attempt to foster a sense of intimacy between separated partners, which she feels modern communication systems deny.

Her project Absent, 2004, is a series of accessories or "connecting pieces", which each combine a garment, such as a tie or underwear, with a ring or a necklace. When a couple purchase a pair of accessories, the jewellery is enclosed inside the garment and heat pressed so as to leave an embossed pattern on the surface of the fabric. Hayashi hopes that when apart, this will allow the lovers to share the memory of the object, as if connected through it. The pattern left can provide a trace on to which to project their thoughts and memories of one another, encouraging stories of intimacy to be fabricated in the absence of the real thing.

The imprint left by the jewellery will gradually disappear — physically marking the time spent apart and suggesting the fading of memories themselves — to be recreated when the couple reunite. Whilst highly conceptual, Hayashi's pieces rely largely for their effects on their tactility. To this end, she has chosen to use pure silk organza for the garments, in order to evoke the touch of skin to skin and so enhance the sense of closeness between the couple. This sheer, delicate fabric, at once sensual and fragile, evokes the intimacy felt between lovers, and symbolises their temporary loss of one another.

1 Absent 04, 2004, silver and silk organza, ring: 3 x 3 cm, tie: 1 x 10 cm

2 Absent 01-1, 2004, silver and silk organza, undergarment: 13 x 10 cm; ring: 3 x 3 cm

3 Absent 01-2, 2004, silver and silk organza, 15 x 15 cm

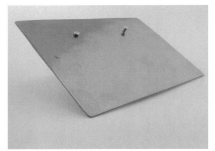

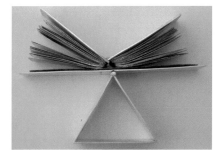
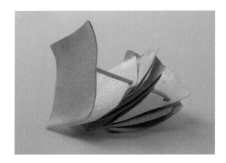

Alyssa Dee Krauss

Rather than approaching jewellery as ornament, Alyssa Dee Krauss attempts to create a symbol of the constant evolution and flux of life, using the book as a metaphor for this ongoing process. The idea that jewellery embodies fixed ideals is, she contends, a misrepresentation of the way in which a piece changes with its wearer, continually imbued with new memories and new meanings. Dee Krauss describes her Bindings series, 2002, as a "'precious' collection of wearable bound objects whose pages perpetually archive and retell the tales chosen for them". In this series, gold and silver rings are comprised of layers, or 'leaves'. Some, such as The Book of Impossible Choices, Volume II, 2002, overtly reference the book format, whereas others such as The Book of Empty Promises, Volume II and The Book of Almosts, both 2002, abstract the form of book leaves into multiple layers of symbolic shapes, expressing her aim to "weave together archetypal constructions, forms and concepts to create truly personal objects from universal components".

Works such as The Book of Unreturned Letters, 2002, retain the shape of the page more explicitly, the leaves piled on top of each other as if waiting for new stories to be inscribed on their surface. Dee Krauss also creates an expectancy of further narrative with her use of titles, which although very suggestive have no explanation in the pieces themselves. Much like a book that has not yet been written, these small scale works gradually unfold, inviting meaning to be given by the individual wearer.

1 The Ring that Binds series: The Book of Empty Promises, Volume II, ring, 2002, 18 ct yellow and white gold

2 The Book of Pride, brooch, 2002, steel, glass and thread

3 The Ring that Binds series: The Book of... Let Me Count the Ways, 2002, 18 ct gold

4 The Book of Impossible Choices, Volume II, ring, 2002, sterling silver

5 The Book of Unreturned Letters, ring, 2002, sterling silver

Francisca Kweitel

Francisca Kweitel's politically engaged brooches present, on displays shaped like slide mounts, "apocalyptic visions" of "destructions, hopelessness, disagreements, fights of power and irrefutable beliefs", in the hope that exposure of these issues and her insistence on engaging with them through wear, will mean that they are not forgotten. As well as her hopes for the wearer or "holder" of her work to engage, Kweitel hopes for a kind of catharsis for herself, as a relief from her intense involvement with Buenos Aires' — her home city — troubles, as if their materialisation in miniature helps her to make them manageable.

In this way, there is a tension in her work. Caught between wanting to tell unheard stories and a sense of despair and desire to retreat, her jewellery appears as neither fact nor fiction, combining material from the everyday and the political with the delicacy, symbols and scale of the imagination.

She quotes Paul Auster:
"When you don't even have the hope of regaining hope, you tend to fill the empty spaces with dreams, small fantasies that help you to survive."

1 Always there…, 2004, brooch, sterling silver, newspaper and sequins, 5 x 5 cm

2 Not everything that shines is gold, 2004, brooch, silver, paper and acrylic paint, 5 x 5 cm

Hannah Louise Lamb

Relating her early work to Cornwall and the coastal imagery of her childhood, Hannah Louise Lamb has continued to develop a broader language to evoke the familiarity and comfort that we associate with home. Using a simple outline of a house, natural forms, and widely recognisable domestic imagery and colouring, Lamb creates a template onto which we can project our personal memories and fantasies of home. In the brooch, Tremonck, 2004, a shape reminiscent of a photo frame invites us to imagine a family member or friend pictured inside, allowing us to reflect on our own sense of place and belonging. The brooch makes use of a piece of porcelain from the beach by her home, but is also intended to recall china that she dug up from her garden as a child. In this way, her work is constructed from disparate fragments of the past and conceptually located in different places, conveying the complex layers of our associations of home.

Lamb's work is characterised by this innovative use of materials. Stock domestic fabrics such as porcelain, silk and wallpaper evoke nostalgia, and combine with delicate silver shapes and silhouettes, beads and soft pastel colours to remind us of the precious, even fragile nature of memories themselves.

1 Bobby, brooch, 2004, silver, pearl and quartz,
8 x 5 x 0.6 cm

2 Home, brooches and bangles, 2004, silver, felt and silk, 6 x 8.2 x 1 cm each

3 Suburbia, necklace, 2004, silver, 45 x 1.8 cm

4 Tremonck, brooch, 2004, silver and porcelain,
6 x 4 x 0.7 cm

Laura Potter

Playing with common perceptions of jewellery as decorative art,
Laura Potter invites us to look at her pieces as 'precious' in a
different sense, as key artifacts in the establishment of identity
and as integral to our everyday habits. Concentrating on the idea
communicated, she uses a variety of materials, drawing on the
visual and conceptual language of the domestic, incorporating, for
example, a gold ring and a brass padlock photographed around a
bathroom tap in Untitled (locked), 2004. In this piece the ring is
locked to the tap and is only made functional as jewellery in its
sequel piece, Untitled (unlocked), 2004, which involves unlocking
the ring so that it can be worn. Using familiar imagery and themes
of marital commitment and responsibility as in these pieces, Potter
draws attention to the potential of jewellery to communicate that
which is most close to home.

Whilst her earlier work was concerned with jewellery as a medium
to expose the practices of everyday life, significant in Potter's recent
work is also the sense in which her pieces can actively shape
our individual stories, commemorating and interpreting particular
moments through their wear. Joint Custody, 2003, a gold necklace
with the tags 'Mum' and 'Dad' that can be worn interchangeably,
exemplifies this dual intention: testimony to an event in a family's
story, the necklaces simultaneously help navigate such an event with
a characteristic wit and playfulness. The piece is evidence of Potter's
attempt to create "jewellery as muse".

"Personal possessions are integral to the way an individual
constructs an identity: we compose and communicate who we
are through the things we have."

1	2	3
4	5	

1 Upset Rings, 2003, silver,
2 cm diameter, photography:
L Cheung

2 Locket Cam, pinhole
camera locket, 2003, silver,
4.5 cm diameter, photography:
L Cheung

3 Untitled (locked), ring,
2004, gold, adapted padlock,
ring: 2.5 cm diameter,
padlock: 2 x 2 x 1 cm,
photography: L Cheung

4 Flocked Locket, 2003,
silver and nylon fibre flock,
2.5 x 2 cm, photography:
Laura Potter

5 Untitled (unlocked), ring,
2004, gold, 2.5 cm diameter,
photography: L Cheung

Hans Stofer

Playfully manipulating found objects, Hans Stofer uses the strange and the unforeseen to transform personal adornment. Commonplace items such as a key or a light bulb are wittily altered to create visual conundrums and produce unexpected associations. Drawing on surrealist imagery, many pieces combine incongruous objects as visual clues — reminiscent of the work of Joseph Cornell — but to what, exactly, remains unclear. Narratives may be suggested but are left for the wearer to imagine, providing an opportunity for self-expression and exploration of identity.

"We are naturally attracted to certain objects. We express and define ourselves through these. But it is also us who give objects meaning."

To this end, many of Stofer's pieces require direct involvement. For example in Sleeping Beauty, 1999-2004, a ring has been assembled inside a light bulb. To access and wear the ring the bulb has to be broken, encouraging the performance of meaning through physical engagement. However, as critic Ralph Turner has observed, the work often has a "sting in its tail". Love, 2002-2004, is a tiny key which Stofer suggests is worn on a string around the neck, fragile and vulnerable with a rose thorn on its end, thwarting use and giving what should be a pretty keepsake an air of melancholy. This piece exemplifies Stofer's desire to question received cultural values, an attitude he acknowledges as owing much to the anti-art movement Dada.

1 Hand on My Heart (detail), hand brooch, 2004, plastic snake and wood, photography: Patrick Letschka

2 Love, 2002-2004, steel key and rose thorn, photography: Patrick Letschka

3 Mr Gold, convention badge, 2004, PVC convention badge, plastic bag, rivets, fine gold, masking tape, photography: Patrick Letschka

4 Cross My Heart, necklace, 2004, fine silver, stainless steel and ball chain, photography: Patrick Letschka

5 Sponge Finger, ring, 2002, aluminium, stainless steel, mild steel and sponge stone, photography: Holly Jolliffe

6 Hermes Of The Spirit, mourning necklace, 2001/2004-ongoing, sapphires, gold, cotton, needle, glass, paper, etc., photography: Hans Stofer

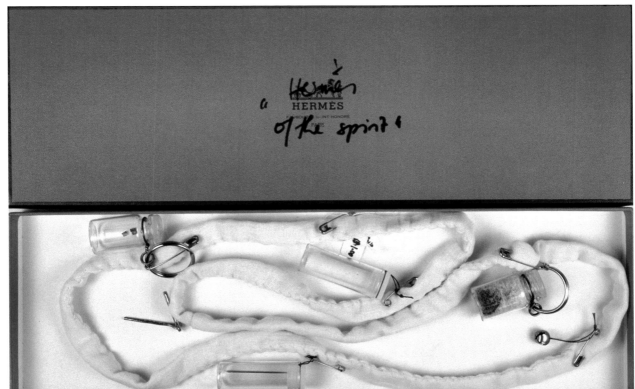

Harriet Clayton
Sarah Crawford
Nicolas Estrada
Melanie Hall
Sarah King
Sarah Lindsay
Marlene McKibbin
Tom Mehew
Kathie Murphy
Adam Paxon
Kaz Robertson
Anoush Waddington

COLOUR AND LIGHT

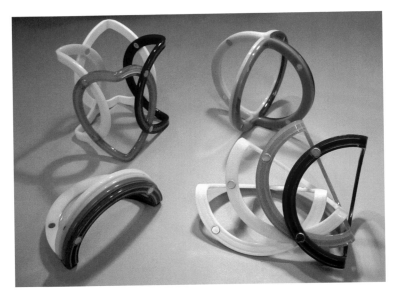

Harriet Clayton

Harriet Clayton's work draws on a number of design influences, with her bold forms recalling ancient Egypt as much as 1960s pop in their shapes, colour and use of materials. Her aesthetic is both fun and glamorous, as much at home with bright primaries as with gold and Swarovski crystal, all of which are incorporated in her assertive designs. This combination has led to a number of private and press commissions for oversize visors and headpieces, calling upon her sense of the decorative and theatrical; the same approach informs Clayton's highly wearable seasonal collections. Early collections include playful, colourful multi-way bracelets based on cut-out discs, hoops and hemispheres; whilst recent collections have featured elegant cuffs and rings in lustrous cut-away gold, their curving, pointed structures capturing and reflecting light.

Using laser cutting and etching, as well as heat forming techniques, she has become known for her uniquely worked acrylic surfaces; by adding contrasting colour inlays, and also recently experimenting with precious metals and leather, the pieces have an intricacy and depth which complements the strong, rigid forms.

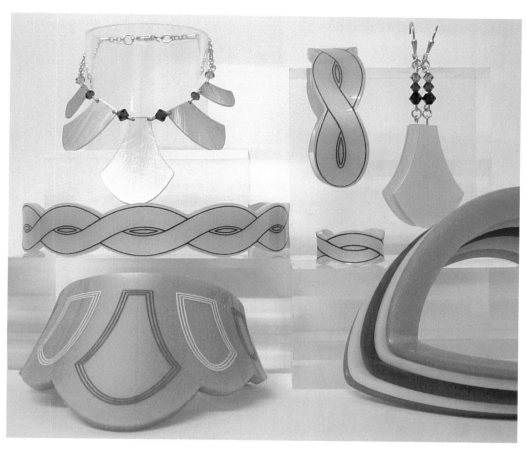

1 Ball Bangles, 2003, acrylic
and magnets, 10 x 5 cm

2 Circle and Disc Earring,
2003, acrylic and silver,
13 cm

3 Spring/Summer collection,
2004, silver, rings 2 cm
diameter, cuffs 7 x 5 cm

4 Autumn/Winter collection,
2004, acrylic, silver,
and Swarovski crystal,
various sizes

5 Grace cuff, 2004,
gold-plated silver, 7 x 5 cm

Sarah Crawford

An innovative, tactile designer, Sarah Crawford insists on using hand-tool based methods in her work, to allow herself the greatest possible scope for freedom to experiment. She invents modes of construction as she creates; currently working with sheets and strips of acrylic and Formica, she 'plays' with her materials, folding, weaving and joining to form stronger and more 'lively' panels which are then made into the final objects. Interested in notions of use and context, Crawford allows the briefs she receives for commissions and exhibitions to feed into her technique.

The pieces themselves, with their playful references to fruit, flowers and animals, and their bright, chunky forms, grow directly from these evolving construction methods. By joining, manipulating and layering, Crawford creates engaging and appealing textures, patterns and shapes — bright red, freshly-sliced tomato, richly layered tiger's eye, perfectly circular periwinkle-blue flowers — all characterised by a seductive, glossy finish.

"When I play with my materials it is fun that I take seriously. When I make objects I play in a silly way."

"I consider the pieces I make as exhibition or art pieces, not everyday accessories."

1 Lobe Gardening, 2003, layered acrylic, Formica, magnets and silver

2 Salad Brooch, 2004, layered acrylic, Formica, magnets and silver

3 Tiger Lil, 2004, layered acrylic, Formica and silver

4 Window Box Brooch, 2004, layered acrylic, Formica and silver

5 Special Tweet, 2004, carved Formica solid surfacing

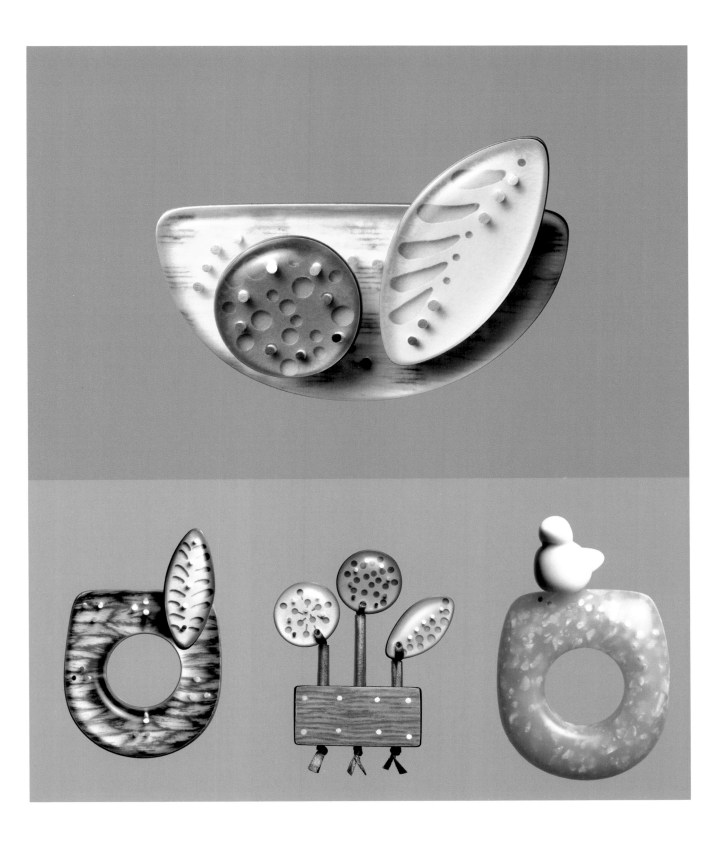

1 | 2

3

1 Scapular 1, necklace,
2004, silver, plastic, paper
and thread, 2 x 2 cm

2 Tapunami's Secret,
necklace, 2003, vegetable
ivory, silver and electronic
components, 6 x 4 x 3 cm

3 Bright Star, necklace, 2004,
tropical seed, gold, silver
and electronic components,
8 x 6.5 x 3 cm

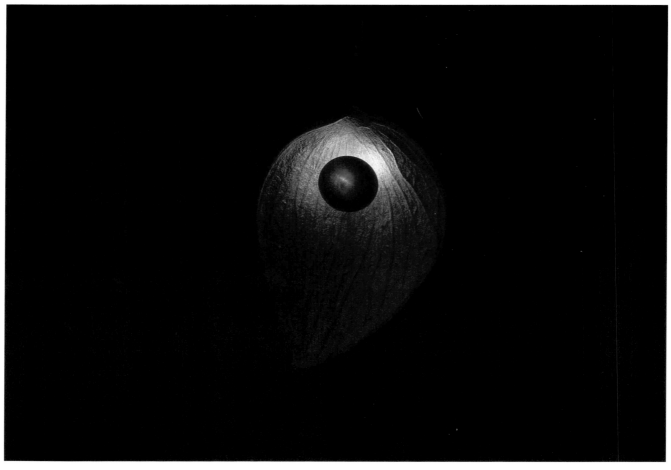

Nicolas Estrada

Colombian-born Nicolas Estrada is now based in Barcelona, where
he learned his craft. He continues to find inspiration from his
home country, in particular from the legends of the Colombian Native
Indians. Drawing upon the creation myths surrounding the sun, moon,
earth and stars, his jewellery often contain their own light sources,
combining electronic components with more traditional elements. In
this mixing of precious stones and metals with lights and also with
organic materials such as exotic seeds, many of his works have an
ethereal, magical quality. This contrasts with his more explicitly
political jewellery, such as Scapular 1, 2004, which comments on
the relationship between traditional religion and violence. Estrada
engages with the natural world, the physical body, and philosophy
and culture in equal measure, to create beautiful, mysterious and
sensual pieces.

"It is the creation of a new world where light and legend
are combined."

Melanie Hall

Melanie Hall works mainly in plastic with silver or silver-plated copper to create her vibrant pieces. She is interested in the interaction of "the wearer and the piece and the rest of the world", often using components which create sound with the movement of the body, and cast shadows or reflect colour on to the skin. Her jewellery use simple flower shapes in brilliant colours, which when combined and repeated with fine silver wires become ebullient, blooming adornments. While her colour schemes and concepts are highly contemporary, she is interested in engaging with traditional materials and forms, so that the bright plastic is set off by the delicacy of the metallic structure; boldness by a subtlety perfect for elegant but striking evening wear.

Her recent work with lettered plastic strips demonstrates further her witty, personal approach, exploring an alternative to her transparent flower forms in a collection which allows her to personalise each piece for the wearer. Creating a message specific to them, this statement becomes a surreal but subtle element of the jewellery's design — as in enigmatic Stroke the Voluptuous Fur.

1 Flower Neckpiece, 2004,
plastic and silver, 20 x 25
cm, photography: Iain Jones

2 Twist Me, Turn Me, 2004,
plastic and silver-plated
copper, 20 x 25 cm,
photography: Iain Jones

3 Flower Necklace 2, 2004,
plastic and silver,
20 x 25 cm, photography:
Holly Jolliffe

4 Stroke the Voluptuous Fur,
2004, plastic and silver,
22 x 26 cm, photography:
Iain Jones

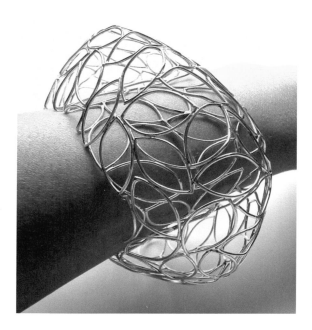

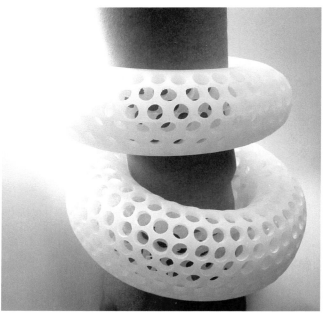

Sarah King

"I'm fascinated by the way other makers have pioneered plastics in jewellery, but I think my main inspiration comes from fine art and architecture."

King's work explores ideas of space, absence and transparency. She is intrigued by what is left unsaid and the infinite possibility that emerges from this silence. King's time spent studying sculpture at Goldsmiths College is a major influence in her work, constructing her pieces as sculpture, utilising materials such as African blackwood and resin mixed with more traditional jewellery materials such as silver and pearls.

In the 2003 series, Light Constructions, rings and outsize bangles are created from silver or white and transparent resins, exploring qualities of structure and hollowness. The large scale of her jewellery contrasts with the open metal work and translucency of the plastics used, playing against the skin of the wearer, with the lightness of the pieces stopping them from being overwhelming. Through her work, King has specialised in mixing precious and non-precious materials such as carved wood with silver and pearls, or frosted resin with silver, approaching these materials in the same way as she mixes structure with space.

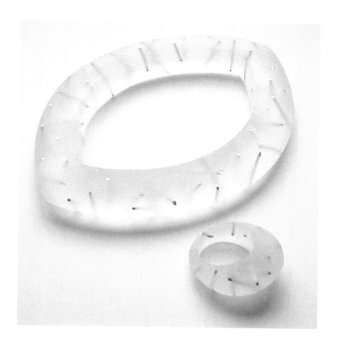

1 Light Constructions
Bracelet, 2003, sterling silver,
8 x 7 x 13 cm

2 Light Constructions
Bracelets, 2003, resin,
8 x 6 x 14 cm

3 Light Constructions
Bracelet and Ring, 2003,
resin and sterling silver,
bracelet 3 x 12 x 9 cm,
ring 3 x 2.5 x 4 cm

4 Light Constructions Ring,
2003, sterling silver,
4.5 x 4 x 5 cm

5 Wood and Pearl Rings,
2002, African blackwood and
pearls, 3.5 x 3.5 x 5 cm

1	2
	3

1 Dust Loops Necklace,
2003, acrylic, nylon and
silver, 58 cm, photography:
Holly Jolliffe

2 Dust Necklace, 2004,
acrylic, styrene and nylon,
5 x 70 x 0.1 cm

3 Dust Bangles, 2004,
acrylic, 6 x 6.5 x 0.3 cm

Sarah Lindsay

Sarah Lindsay uses a heat-press to form varied composites from off-cuts of plastic, creating a new, delicate material, perfectly complemented by her pretty yet bold designs. Colours mix and combine organically through this process, with Lindsay leaving the edges unfinished, using technology to create organic form. She treads a line between these two poles, the hi-tech and the natural.

Lindsay claims that the "speckled surfaces" which result from her method remind her of "flickering pixels on a computer screen", an inspiration which she pursues in, for example, her long, slender, elegant brooches, made up of many tiny squares of blue, turquoise and green. Other pieces in her recent Dust Collection, 2003-2004, are formed of luminescent discs, reminiscent of agate slices in their rough edges and intense variegation of colour. There is a high degree of wearability in Lindsay's work, as she aims for a soft, lightweight quality "which has an empathy with textiles".

"My craft is inspired by the visual sensation of technology whilst the low-tech processes I use keep me in physical contact with materials."

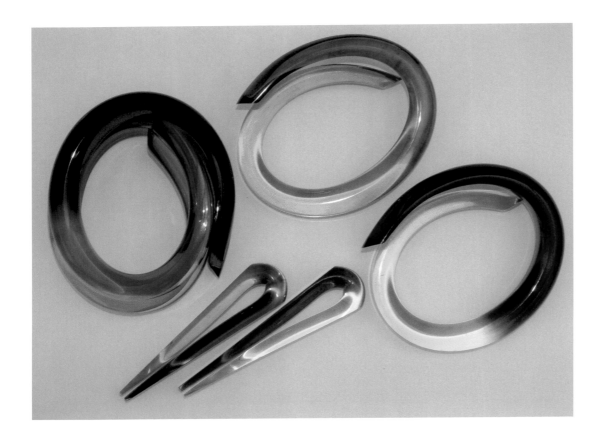

Marlene McKibbin

Since the mid 1970s, Marlene McKibbin has been making jewellery in a wide variety of materials. Following an essentially modernist aesthetic, her designs are very simple in form, with her minimalist sense of proportion informing all her work over the course of a long and varied career.

The main body of her work has been in acrylic, although lately she has been working in stainless steel. Acrylic allows her to mould clear planes of material into elegant shapes, which she then decorates with colourful, simple patterns, heating the plastic and bending it to shape before colouring with dyes which remain impregnated in the surface. She is not averse to bold colour and has used luminous pinks, yellows, and greens in much of her work. Her recent work in stainless steel, in which curving ladder forms predominate, show her continuing interest in the interaction of surface and light.

"Visually and structurally I strive to achieve rhythm by the simplest possible means."

1 'e' Bangles and Peg Brooches, 2004, dyed acrylic, bangles 10 x 85 x 25 cm, pegs 10 x 25 x 12 cm

2 Turned Bangles, 1991, acrylic, 14.5 x 10.5 x 2.5 cm, 13.5 x 9 x 2 cm

3 Drilled and Threaded Bangles, 1978, acrylic and embroidery silk thread, 9 x 9 x 1.5 cm

4 Three Bud Necklace with Bud Pins, 2002, stainless steel, gold and porcupine quills, pin 5 x 18 x 0.2 cm, necklace 3 x 40 x 0.2 cm

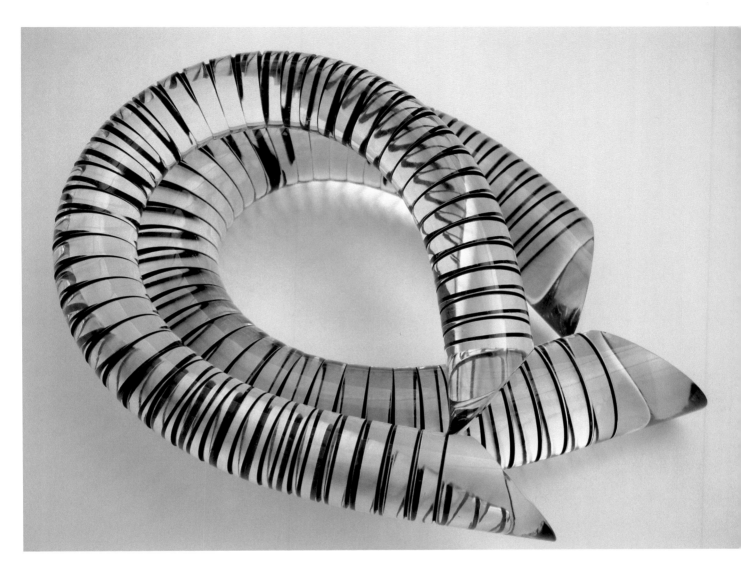

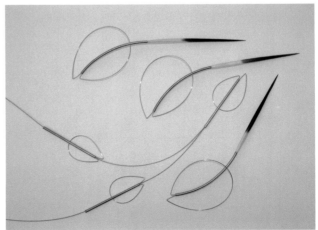

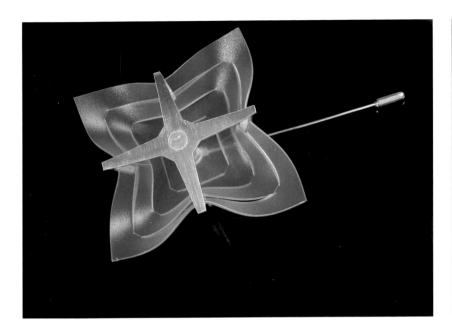

Tom Mehew

Tom Mehew manipulates polypropylene sheets into structured, three-dimensional shapes, with his sensitive gathers and folds creating organic floral forms. The richness of the colours work with the lightweight quality of the material, so that the darkness of the cut edges offsets the translucent 'petals' as light passes through. The central rods, which become a part of the attachment in his brooch designs, create a focal point around which the shape grows. Making use of the highest quality synthetics and industrial design, the delicacy of Mehew's brooches and corsages embody a love of traditional form married to a mastery of modern technique.

His success since graduating in 2001 has opened the way to a range of other design activities, and Mehew has applied his innovative, versatile techniques to homewares and lighting design, allowing him to fully exploit the potential of his materials and methods, and further explore the relationship between the buyer and the design.

"The concept of my work stems from forms I created by folding Travelcards on my way to college, seeing how many shapes I could make from one ticket."

1 Fourpoint Brooch, 2002, polypropylene and silver, 6.5 x 6.5 cm

2 Flowform shallow bowl, 2004, silver and gold-plate, 35 x 35 cm

3 Neck-clip Blue Brooch, 2002, polypropylene and silver, 6.5 x 6.5 cm

1 Necklace, 2004, polyester,
resin and thread,
photography: Kathie Murphy

2 Bangles, 2004, polyester,
resin and thread,
photography: Holly Jolliffe

Kathie Murphy

Working in polyester resin allows Kathie Murphy to experiment with both colour and opacity, mixing a kaleidoscopic palette with a range of transparencies and solid colour. Simple forms belie a complexity of colour combinations: bright, lucent aquamarines sitting alongside delicate peaches and peppermints, with networks of threads suspended in the resin giving the jewellery an unusual texture, mixing brilliant hues with pale tints. She enjoys using repetitive forms which, when collected together, make something tactile and bold. She looks to her own childhood for inspiration — she recalls, as a six year-old, the "continuing fascination" of endless colour combinations — and to a diverse collection of other sources. Simplifying the shapes of musical instruments, glyphs and letters into abstract forms has led her to incorporate cut-out metal components along with flat, bright resin pieces, while the assembly of small, spiky, brown and green threads in other work recalls both plant life, and modernist sculptors such as Jean Tinguely, who Murphy identifies as an influence.

"My jewellery combines material, shape and colour to produce pieces that are amusing and tactile."

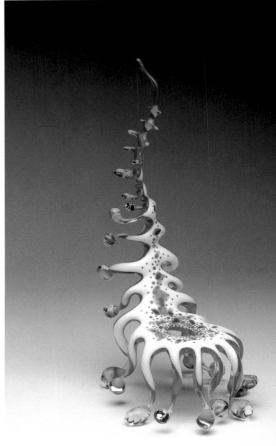

Adam Paxon

Adam Paxon works with acrylic, blending his own colours, laminating, carving and refining to create his distinctive, glistening pieces. He is as much interested in the effects of light as he is in the unique palette he has developed, exploring the possibilities of reflection and transparency in his work. At times, as in his ear-pins, coloured light is reflected through the jewellery onto skin or cloth. This attention to the relationship between wearer and jewellery informs the use of hidden and enclosed attachments, so that his organic forms are not interrupted.

The work is full of life, and imbued with a playful quality; by using springs and moving parts, Paxon makes pieces which seem to be "breathing, quivering, or foraging". Reminiscent of flowers and insects, there is a fecundity, a sensuousness and at times an eroticism to Paxon's forms, as he says "as if about to burst with ripeness".

"... as pieces develop I see them becoming more and more like creatures to wear".

"I've attempted to give the impression that these pieces have grown or erupted out of the garment... or are resting on it and perhaps about to scurry over the shoulder."

1 Mirror Bangle, 2003, acrylic, 12 cm diameter

2 Adrenaline, 2003, acrylic and polyester, 28.5 cm

photography: Graham Lees

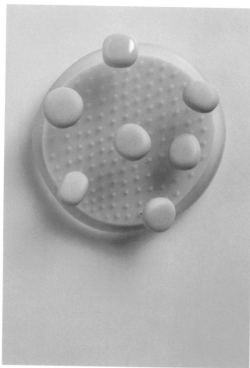

1 Custard and Cubes Brooch, 2003, resin, magnets and nylon wire

2 Sticky Pink Brooch, 2003, resin, magnets and steel wire

3 Square Rings, 2003, resin

photography: John K McGregor

Kaz Robertson

Kaz Robertson utilises the versatility of resin to add a depth and richness to her candy coloured work. Layering patterns on solid and transparent planes of colour, she builds up a density of effect that engages with the light reflecting and absorbing qualities of her material. This playfulness and adaptability in the making process extends to her design concept; Robertson emphasises 'playability', with the use of magnets, reversibility, and add-on parts allowing the wearer to "stick and shake" their pieces and "watch them wobble". The base part of a ring or brooch can be worn alone, or dressed up with the addition of extra magnetic parts to create something more extravagant; reversible pieces have a subtle and a daring side; colours and sizes are endlessly interchangeable. Robertson's palette of lime green, bubblegum pink, fuschia, white and baby blue complement her sense of fun, while the simple but slightly irregular rectangles, hoops, discs and squares of her bracelets, rings and brooches, stuck with bobbles standing away from the surfaces, reinforce her informal approach. Robertson explains her method of jewellery making as follows: "Interaction and versatility are two of the most important aspects of my work... I perceive each piece as a wearable toy."

1 Orange Wings, 2003,
polypropylene, silver,
Swarovski crystal and
stainless steel, 60 x
50 x 60 cm diameter,
photography: David Willis

2 Pink Heart Pin, 2004,
polypropylene, silver,
swarovski crystal,
stainless steel and beads,
7 x 6 x 2.5 cm

3 Autumn Collar, 2004,
polypropylene, silver,
Swarovski crystal and
stainless steel, 40 x 30 x
45 cm diameter, photography:
David Willis

4 Purple Gemset Ring, 2004,
polypropylene, silver, cubic
zircon, Swarovski crystal
and beads, 6 x 6 x 4 cm

Anoush Waddington

"Whenever I am working on a new design I consider the suitability of the materials and their characteristics, rather than their intrinsic value. A designer should be free to combine a range of elements into their final piece."

A passion for adornment and fashion inspires Waddington's work, reflected in collaborations with a variety of fashion designers, as well as projects in interior design, millinery and accessories. The vibrant colours of her birthplace, Sao Paolo and the energy of Brazilian music are big influences on her work, which utilises strong colours accentuated by gemstones. Working with her partner who is a steelsmith and metal jeweller, Waddington has developed a range of techniques for using polypropylene, a lightweight colourful material, combining it with more traditional silverwork. Purple Gemset Ring, 2004 is representative of her use of colour and a starburst motif that reoccurs in many of her pieces. This motif is explored using a number of different references, including snowflakes, flowers or hearts, as in White Flake Pin, 2004, and Pink Heart Pin, 2004.

"It is essential that each piece should compliment the body, emphasising the line and shape, utilising space, form and colour."

Kathleen Bailey
Donna Barry
Peter Chang
Gerda Flöckinger
Anna Lewis
Lynne Kirstin Murray
Axel Russmeyer

DECORATIVE ELEMENTS

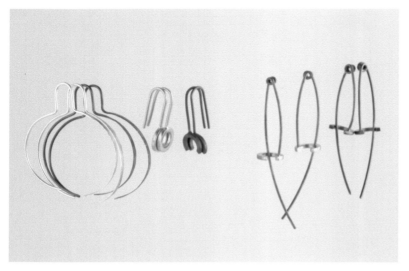

Kathleen Bailey

Using everyday materials and objects as her starting point, Kathleen Bailey draws upon the fastening mechanisms and modes of production in her jewellery to find new, innovative forms. Her Sugar Crystal jewellery, begun in 2003, are rings that are intended to be used as utensils in a recipe that forms the colourful gemlike forms from sugar on the silver support, while the Silver Shape Collection, begun in 2002, uses staple fastenings as a point of departure. The Relic collection, 2004, mixes silver with gold, using diamonds "like subtle punctuation marks". The collection takes its inspiration from archaeological finds, the oxidised silver emulating the striations and erosions of time upon ancient jewellery pieces. The fastenings also imitate historical structures; toga pins are featured as works in their own right as well as being used as mechanisms for fastening for other pieces, and necklaces and bracelets are fastened by solid loops and hanging chains. Bringing the source into a contemporary context, the forms of these pieces reference both Roman and punk cultures.

"My work is influenced by a pre-occupation with traditional jewellery ... [and] a desire to rework or find an alternative method for securing a piece to the body".

1 Relic earrings, hoops, hooks and pins, 2004, silver, oxidised silver and 18 ct gold

2 Relic rings set, 2004, silver, oxidised silver, 18 ct gold and diamonds

3 Relic rings, detail, 2004, silver, gold and oxidised silver

4 Relic enamelled rings, 2004, silver, oxidised silver and enamelling

5 Relic reconstructed tube ring, 2004, silver tube, etching, enamelling and 18 ct gold

Donna Barry

Working with scraps of silver and gold, Donna Barry's personal technique involves the fusing of precious metals into textured sheets. She overlaps simple shapes to create repetitive patterns, which can be worked to varying degrees of complexity; as a maker, there is a playful aspect to her method that allows her to experiment with this basic technique and find endless new patterns and forms. Her work is light and tactile, the layering and cutting creating a sense of fragility and delicacy. Layers and folds of the fine metallic surface glint at different angles; often incorporating movable elements which respond to the wearer, these are pieces suffused with light and life.

Barry draws upon the patterning found in natural forms, such as flowers and fish scales, as well as tiling and other manmade surfaces. She uses the same techniques to create dishes and silverware, a maker clearly creating work to be enjoyed as one might a favourite heirloom: too lovely not to be shown off, worn and used.

"Arranging shapes into patterns, the flat construction of sheet is transformed when it becomes three-dimensional. Only once the pieces are completed do they become familiar."

1	2	3
4	5	

1 Daisy Chain, 2003, silver and 18 ct gold, photography: John K McGregor

2 Three Lily Brooch, 2003, silver, photography: John K McGregor

3 Criss Cross Dish, 2003, silver and 18 ct yellow gold, 8 x 8 cm

4 Series of floral rings, 2003, oxidised silver, silver, 18 ct red and yellow gold

5 Floral Cup Bed Brooch, 2003, silver and 18 ct yellow gold

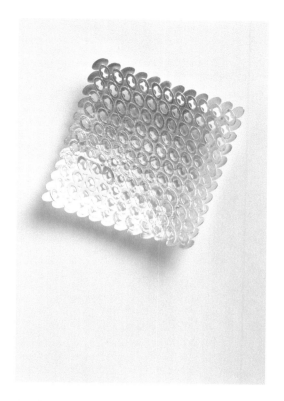

Peter Chang

Peter Chang is both a sculptor and jeweller, with his jewellery bearing the influence of his broader work in three-dimensional form. His work is both fantastic and rooted in his observation of what surrounds us, realised through a range of complex techniques which he has developed over the course of a long and diverse career. Working almost exclusively in acrylic, Chang sculpts this manmade material as if it were precious gemstones, as well as incorporating found objects into his oversized bangles and brooches.

An intensity of colour is brought out and complemented by the almost liquid sheen of his highly textured pieces, with the intricate patterning that characterises his work highlighted by the introduction of glitter and gold. Detailed, vibrant sculpted form is combined with shaped curves made out of acrylic, resin and metallic elements. Distinctive and complex shapes are built around the basic circular form; butterflies and larvae seem to morph into motorbike and car parts. Gelling together into one fascinating semi-organic structure, his jewellery seem to have come to rest or curled themselves independently around the body of the wearer.

1 Untitled Ring, 2003, acrylic, resin, silver and gold, 5.4 x 4.6 x 2.6 cm, photography: Peter Chang

2 Hamburg Bracelet, 2003, acrylic, resin and silver, 15 x 16.5 x 7.8 cm, photography: Peter Chang

3 Fontinella III Brooch, 2003, acrylic, resin and silver, 12.2 x 6 x 1.5 cm, photography: Peter Chang

4 Fontinella I Bracelet, 2002, acrylic and resin, 16.7 cm outside diameter x 6.8 cm, photography: Shannon Tofts

Gerda Flöckinger

Eminent artist Gerda Flöckinger has been creating innovative work since the 1950s, whose influence has been felt throughout subsequent decades of jewellery practice. Over the course of a prolific and remarkable career, she has established herself as a maker of jewels that are rare and rich in both technique and appearance.

A pioneer in method as well as design, she was among the first makers to use non-precious materials such as wooden beads, seedpods and copper in some of her early work. During the 1960s Flöckinger was asked by the Principal of Hornsey College of Art (now Middlesex University) to set up an experimental jewellery course, which was to influence generations of jewellery practice in the UK and beyond, with Flöckinger's background in fine art underlying her approach to design. Her work was to prove influential in establishing a highly productive dialogue between jewellery and fine art.

In the early 1960s Flöckinger began to develop some of the fusion techniques which she has continued to augment and which remain an essential part of all her work since; the technique has been refined but the pieces retain the same almost organic, twisting, complex forms, using precious metals in combination with cabochons, coloured diamonds and pearls. Flöckinger uses an improvisational approach to making her pieces, starting at times from a multitude of sketches, then working intuitively with the materials in a process that she has described as both composing and performing at the same time.

"The technique is one of total risk at all times — of total melt-down or irreparable damage. The secret is to keep just on the edge of that, and stay there." Tanya Harrod

1 Ring, 1991, 18 ct gold and Indian Moonstone

2 Cufflink, 1990, oxidised silver, 18 ct gold, cultured coloured pearls and brown diamonds

3 Group of three rings, 1994, 18 ct gold with pink cabochon tourmaline; 18 ct gold with small diamonds and holes; 18 ct gold with three grey cultured pearls, diamond disc and plain gold disc

4 Bracelet, 1994, 18 ct gold with blue/grey and white cultured pearls, pink, grey, lilac, orange, brown and blue diamonds, gold disc and two gold tails and cabochon amethyst

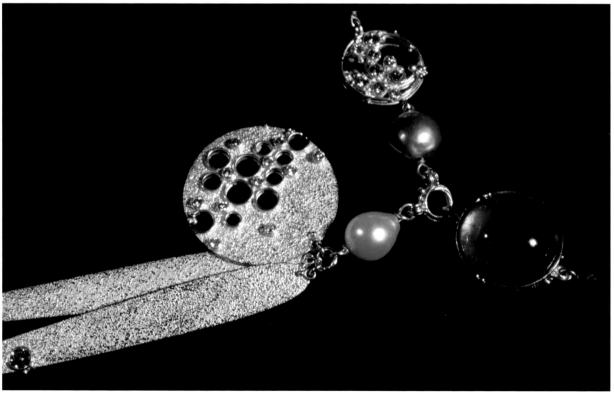

| 1 | 2 |
| 3 | 4 |

1 Vanished, wrap, 2003, printed goose feathers, invisible thread, 150 x 25 cm, photography: Jesse Seaward

2 Silver and Printed Feather Necklace, 2003, printed goose feathers, silver, 21 cm, photography: Anna Lewis

3 Pin Tuffs, 2003, printed goose feathers, silver, 9 cm, photography: Jesse Seaward

4 Trace, neckpiece, 2002, printed goose feathers, crin and wire, 40 x 30 cm, photography: Jesse Seaward

model: Jasmine Lewis

Anna Lewis

Anna Lewis uses feathers, sometimes printed, sometimes in their natural state, held together with fine wires and nylon filament to create her fragile, delicate pieces. Feathers are bound together into single flower-like forms, or layered into a fine mesh and wrapped around the neck, down the back, and about the body like blankets or wings. Her work provokes a personal, emotional response in the viewer by using the maker's own autobiographical material. Sources for the traces of imagery she prints onto her pieces include letters, photographs, postcards, butterfly wings, petals, lace, maps and keepsakes, the lightness of the material juxtaposed with the weight of association and remembrance.

Lewis's work ranges from complex, stunning exhibition pieces which enfold the body or appear to hang on the air, to highly wearable chokers, necklaces, rings, earrings and pins. These smaller pieces, combining feathers with leather, silver, and Swarovski crystal, can be made to commission for the individual wearer.

"... my work evokes memory by expressing delicate, ghost-like and ephemeral qualities which allude to the fragile and transient nature of memory... using the feather as a symbolic material (a feather is said to be a measure of your soul)".

"I feel my work crosses some boundaries between art, fashion and jewellery and could be viewed in several different contexts."

1	2
3	4
	5

1 Shake Your Forest
Pom-Poms at Me, 2003,
wood, resin, felt and silver,
12 x 10 x 2 cm

2 Earrings for Munich, 2004,
wood, resin, mixed stones
and silver, 10 x 5 x 2 cm

3 Forest Princess, 2003,
wood, resin, pearls, felt and
silver, 12 x 12 x 30 cm

4 Forest Graffiti Love Nest,
2004, wood, resin, mixed
stones, silver and coral,
10 x 10 x 30 cm

5 Greeny Time, 2004, wood,
resin, mixed stones, silver
and felt, 12 x 8 x 30 cm

Lynne Kirstin Murray

Lynne Kirstin Murray's work is clearly influenced by painting both in style and process. There is spontaneity in the way she creates that is reflected in the free nature of her pieces, commenting that: "My work is full of humour, lively and fresh. I enjoy the scale of my work, the pieces are quite large and dramatic: when worn they definitely make a statement as I think jewellery should do."

Making works in groups, Murray inscribes each with a narrative, linking the work thematically. Many of her pieces have been based on the idea of the forest, as a site for fairytales, as well as a source of natural imagery. Works such as Forest Princess, 2003, draw on the colours and shapes of foliage, with the title of the work implying that the wearer will be transformed into one of Murray's fantasisied characters by putting on the piece. Using a wide range of materials she mixes precious with non-precious, like silver and gold with paint, and felt with wood. The impression is that the construction has the vitality and immediacy of using a brush — as if the pieces have been taken out of a canvas and frozen in three dimensions. Earrings for Munich, 2004 demonstrates this psychedelic juxtaposition of materials, with solid stones of resin in lime and grenadine mixed with turquoise and orange beads.

Axel Russmeyer

Axel Russmeyer's multi-coloured, beaded glass earrings and necklaces
are here shown in his hand-made wooden jewellery boxes, which,
printed with fifteenth century portraits, are as precious as their
contents. Opening to reveal further details of the paintings, with the
typical tracery of fine lines where the paint has cracked with age,
the boxes are in themselves keepsakes, with a sense of delicacy and
decoration that perfectly offsets the jewellery within.

Russmeyer combines tiny seed beads to cover the surface of wooden
spheres, creating pieces with a pleasing textured depth and range of
colour. The labour intensive process involves stringing the beads
over the sphere to create patterned and sometimes multi-coloured
surfaces, with a tonality that references Renaissance costume, further
emphasised by his use of vintage Venetian glass beads alongside
contemporary ones. His palette draws upon the same artworks that
adorn the boxes, muted yet vibrant: deep burnt oranges, ivories,
scarlet, gold, coral, aquamarine, veridian and jet. In both colour
and form, Russmeyer's works evoke heirlooms, stored away in their
precious containers, with the imagery he chooses to frame his
jewellery emphasising their delicate and sumptuous beauty.

1-2 Black Lady Box, 2002,
wood covered with poster
print, stamp and metal
hooks, 40 x 40 x 8 cm
image: Petrus Christus,
Bildnis einer jungen Dame,
c. 1470, large scale poster
printed for the opening of the
new building of the
Gemaeldegalerie Berlin,
Preussicher Kulturbesitz
non matching pair of earrings:
wood, glass and 18 ct gold,
3 cm diameter
set of five necklace sections:
6/7/11/13/17 beaded beads,
wood, glass, resin, metal and
18 ct gold, knotted on ribbon,
1-2.4 cm diameter

3 Classic Beaded Bead
Earring, 2004, size 18
antique Venetian glass beads,
18 ct white gold, polyester
thread and painted wood,
1.8 cm diameter

4 Blue Lady Box, detail of
interior, 2002, wood covered
with poster print, stamp and
metal hooks
image: Antonio del Pallaiuolo,
Profilbildnis einer jugen
Dame, c. 1465-1470, large
scale poster printed as for
Black Lady Box
non matching pair of earrings:
wood, glass and 18 ct gold,
4.5 cm diameter
set of three necklaces:
16/16/21 beaded beads, wood,
glass, resin, metal and 18 ct
gold, knotted on ribbon,
1.4-2.6 cm diameter

photography: Geoff Onyett

BIOGRAPHIES

ORGANIC FORMS

Jane Adam

Born 1954, London, UK, where she lives and works.

Since graduating from Royal College of Art, London, Jane Adam has been working as a freelance jewellery designer exhibiting internationally. From 1997 to 2001 Adam was Senior Research Fellow at the Jewellery Industry Innovation Centre in Birmingham. She was shortlisted for the Jerwood Prize for Applied Arts in 2000, and was founder and Chairman of the Association for Contemporary Jewellery and is currently a trustee of the Crafts Council. Collectors include the Crafts Council, Cooper Hewitt Museum, New York, Carnegie Museum of Art, Pittsburgh, the Victoria & Albert Museum, London.

Selected Exhibitions

2004 Jane Adam (solo exhibition), Scottish Gallery, Edinburgh

2001 Jewellery by the Top Ten, Contemporary Applied Arts, London

2000–2001 Jerwood Prize for Applied Arts: Jewellery, Crafts Council London

Selected Publications

Art and Empire (film), British Galleries, London: Victoria & Albert Museum, 2000.

Crafts magazine, January/February 2000.

Nana Akashi

Born 1975, Tokyo, lives and works in Tokyo, Japan.

Nana Akashi began her studies in product design in Japan, moving to London in 1999 to complete a BA in Jewellery at St Martins College of Art and Design. Following this, Akashi studied at the School of Gemmology in London, before returning to Japan, where she has continued to exhibit her delicate casts of natural forms.

Selected Exhibitions

2004 Significant, Simmon's Gallery, London

2000 The Craft Exhibition, Janome Gallery, Kanazawa, Japan

Katie Clarke

Born 1971 in Stafford, UK, lives and works in Surrey, UK.

Katie Clarke received her BA (Hons) in Jewellery Design from Middlesex University in 1996, and began receiving exhibition offers immediately following her Degree Show. She set up her studio at the Cockpit Arts in London and has since been creating her colourful and sculptural feather jewellery for exhibition, publication, and collection worldwide. Clarke has received international attention through exhibitions in London, Edinburgh, San Francisco, New York, Berlin, and Vienna, and press in The Independent, Cosmopolitan, Harpers and Queen, and The Guardian. Clarke moved her studio in 2004, and is now based in Surrey where she continues to develop her concepts and designs.

Selected Exhibitions

2005 British Craft Trade Fair, Harrogate

2004–2005 Ice White Ferrers Gallery, Staunton Harold

2004–2005 Dazzle, Princes Square, Glasgow; National Theatre, London

Hilde De Decker

Born 1965 in Ghent, lives and works in Ghent.

Hilde De Decker trained in Interior Design and then Jewellery Design from the Sint-Lucas Instituut in Belgium. Her solo exhibitions have mainly been jewellery based but in recent years she has concentrated more on installation work that crosses over between jewellery and fine art. In 1993, Hilde De Decker received the Alessi Award for Silversmithing and was nominated for the Henry de Velde prize for young talent. Since 2000 De Decker has been teaching at the Gerrit Rietveld Academy in Amsterdam. Her work is held in a variety of public collections including the Design Museum in Ghent.

Selected Exhibitions

2004 Lower Gallery, Contemporary Applied Arts, London Mikromegas, Powerhouse Museum, Sydney; John Curtin Gallery, Perth; Oratorio di San Rocco, Padova

2003 Open Borders, Droog Design, Tri Postal, Lille

2001 Belgium-The Netherlands: Jewellery 1945-2000, Design Museum, Ghent

Selected Publications

"New Brutalism", Standaard magazine, April 2004.Art Review, 2003.

Nora Fok

Born 1952, Hong Kong, lives and works in Brighton, UK.

After completing a design degree in Hong Kong, Nora Fok and graduated in Wood, Metal, Ceramics and Plastics from Brighton Polytechnic in 1981. Fok's work is held in the permanent collections of the Contemporary Arts Society, London; Museum für Kunst und Gewerbe, Hamburg and the National Museums of Scotland.

Selected Exhibitions

2004   Body Conscious, Crafts Council at Victoria & Albert Museum, London

2003   J+T Jewellery Meet Textile, Contemporary Applied Arts, London

2001   Mobilia Gallery, Cambridge, MA, USA

Selected Publications

Black, Sandy, Knitwear in Fashion, London: Thames & Hudson, 2001.

Turner, Ralph, The New Jewellery, London: Thames & Hudson, 1985.

Katy Hackney

Born 1967, Dundee, Scotland, lives and works in London, UK.

Having received a first class degree in Jewellery from Edinburgh College of Art, Katy Hackney went on to do an MA at Royal College of Art, London, graduating in 1991. Hackney was recently involved in Collect at the Victoria & Albert Museum, London, as well having exhibited internationally. Her work is held in the collections of The Crafts Council, London, The Royal Museum of Scotland and Montreal Museum of Decorative Arts. Outlets include the Crafts Council shop at the Victoria & Albert Museum and Gill Wing, London, The Scottish Gallery, Edinburgh and Velvet da Vinci, San Francisco, CA.

Selected Exhibitions

2004   Collect, Victoria & Albert Museum, London (represented by Velvet da Vinci, San Francisco, CA)

2001   100% Distilled, New work in Jewellery & Silversmithing from Scotland, Flow, London, toured to Mobilia Gallery, MA; New York School of Interior Design; Velvet da Vinci, San Francisco, CA; Scottish Gallery, Edinburgh

1995   Modern British Jewellery, Landesmuseum, Mainz, Germany

Dorothy Hogg

Born 1945, Troon, lives and works in Edinburgh, Scotland.

Dorothy Hogg studied at Glasgow School of Art, then gained a MA from Royal College of Art, London, in 1970. Hogg received an MBE for services to Jewellery and Silversmithing in 2001. She has been the course leader of the Silversmithing and Jewellery department at the Edinburgh College of Art for 20 years and was appointed professor in 2004. Hogg has exhibited throughout the UK, US and Europe, and had her ten year retrospective at the Scottish Gallery during the Edinburgh Festival in 2004. She has her work in permanent collections at The Royal Museum of Scotland and Musee des arts Decoratifs, Montreal.

Selected Exhibitions

2004   Jewellery Unlimited, Bristol City Art Gallery and Museum

2002   Schmuck, Pinakothek der Moderne, Munich

2001   Artists Jewellery in Contemporary Europe – a Female Perspective, Ilias Lalaounis Jewellery Museum, Athens, Greece

Selected Publications

Oliver, Elizabeth, The Art of Jewellery Design, 2002.

Powers, Alan, Nature in Design, London: Conran Octopus, 2000.

Catalogue for Design in Great Britain exhibition, Cologne, 1997.

Susan Kerr

Born 1980 in Edinburgh, Scotland, lives and works in Livingston, Scotland.

Since gaining a degree in Jewellery and Silversmithing from Edinburgh College of Art in 2003, Susan Kerr has been working as a freelance designer and has exhibited throughout the UK. Kerr was commended in the fashion jewellery category at the 2003 Goldsmith's Craftsmanship and Design Awards. She is currently a part-time artist in residence at Edinburgh College of Art.

Selected Exhibitions

2003-2004 Visual Arts Scotland, Exhibition at the RSA, Edinburgh Designer Jewellers Group, The Barbican Centre, London

2002-2003 Dazzle, National Theatre, London

Selected Publications

"Most Wanted", Sunday Herald Magazine, April 2004.

"Hot Shots", Elle Decoration, July 2003.

The Telegraph Magazine, June 2003.

Beth Legg

Born 1981, Scotland, lives and works in Caithness, Scotland

Having received a first class BA in Design and Applied Arts from Edinburgh College of Arts in 2003, Beth Legg has exhibited and sold her work across the UK. Legg has been the recipient of a variety of awards including the Harley Award for Best Use of Materials, The Helen A Rose Bequest Award, The Worshipful Company of Goldsmiths Craftsmanship and Design Awards and Second Place in New Designer of the Year in 2003. Her work is held in the collections of Francis Raemaekers (Metal Gallery) and the Highland Arts Council.

Selected Exhibitions

2004 Takahiro Kondo, The Scottish Gallery, Edinburgh

2003 Visual Arts Scotland, Royal Society of Arts, Edinburgh
      Dazzle, Royal National Theatre, London

Selected Publications

Crafts magazine, November/December 2003.

Kayo Saito

Born 1969, Yokohama, Japan, lives and works in London.

Educated at London Guildhall and the Royal College of Art, Kayo Saito has since been exhibiting her work internationally. Kaito represented the UK at Inhorgenta in 2000, Munich. She was awarded First Prize in the Bombay Sapphire Martini glass competition and the Innovation award from the British Jewellers Association in 1999. Saito's work is held in the collection of Alice & Louis Koch and is sold at outlets including Normade, Oslo; Galerie Slavik, Vienna and Goed Werk, Brussels.

Selected Exhibitions

2004 SOFT, Asociacion de Creadores Textiles de Madrid, Madrid, Spain
      Collect, Lesley Craze at Victoria & Albert Museum, London

2003 Solo Exhibition, Reverso, Lisbon, Portugal

Mariana Sammartino

Born 1966, Argentina, lives and works in Houston, TX, US.

Having studied industrial design at Colorado Institute of Art, Mariana Sammartino has been working as a freelance jewellery designer in Texas. Over the past 15 years Sammartino has lived and worked in a variety of countries including Europe and North and South America. Her work is sold in Aaron Faber, New York and Velvet da Vinci in San Francisco, CA.

Selected Exhibitions

2004 Visionaries!, Museum of Art and Design, New York, NY
      Joyas, Joias, Latin American Artists, Velvet da Vinci Gallery, San Francisco, CA

2003 About Face, Goldsberry Gallery, Houston, TX

Charlotte De Syllas

Born 1946, Barbados, West Indies, lives and works in London, UK.

Charlotte De Syllas studied at the Hornsey College of Art and was introduced to stone cutting by Gerda Flöckinger and was subsequently self taught. She has lectured at various institutions, including the Royal College of Art, the Victoria & Albert Museum, and the University of the Arts, London. In 1999 De Syllas received the Queen Elizabeth Award for research into glass casting and was awarded the Jerwood Prize in 1995. Her work is in the public collections at Goldsmith's Hall, Crafts Council and the Victoria & Albert Museum, London.

Selected Exhibitions

2004 Collect, Victoria & Albert Museum, London

2000 Treasures of the Twentieth Century, Goldsmith's Hall, London

1996 New Times, New Thinking, Crafts Council, London

Selected Publications

Phillips, Clare, Jewels and Jewellery, London: Victoria & Albert Publications, 2000.

Watkins, David, Design Source Book: Jewellery, London: New Holland, 1999.

Turner, Ralph, Jewelry in Europe and America, London: Thames & Hudson, 1996.

SMALL STATEMENTS

Victoria Archer

Born 1982, Leamington Spa, Warwickshire, UK, lives and works in London, UK.

Victoria Archer gained her BA in Jewellery Design from Central Saint Martins College in London, in 2003.

Selected Exhibitions

2004 New Designers, Business Design Centre, London
Elements, Central Saint Martins College of Art and Design, London

2003 Directions, Central Saint Martins College of Art and Design, London

Gijs Bakker

Born 1942, Amersfoort, The Netherlands, lives and works in Amsterdam, The Netherlands, and Stockholm, Sweden.

Gijs Bakker was trained as a jewellery and industrial designer in Amsterdam at the Gerrit Rietveld Academy, and in Stockholm at the Konstfack Skolan. Bakker's designs include jewellery, home accessories and household appliances, furniture, interiors, public spaces and exhibitions. He co-founded Droog Design in 1993 with Renny Ramakers. Droog is a design studio based on an ever-changing network of international designers and contributes to global design debate. In addition, Bakker has been a professor at The Design Academy in Eindhoven since 1987, and has also lectured at the Design Department of the Academy of Fine Arts in Arnhem and the Delft University of Technology.

Selected Exhibitions

2005 I don't wear jewels, I drive them, Gallery Deuxpoissons, Tokyo

2002 Gijs Bakker Retrospective, Houston Center for Contemporary Craft, Houston, TX

1994 Gijs Bakker: Holes Project, Galerie Spektrum, Munich and Galerie Ra, Amsterdam

Selected Publications

Joris, Yvònne GJM, ed., Jewels of mind and mentality: Dutch jewelry 1950-2000, Amsterdam: 010, 2000.

Bakker, Gijs and Renny Ramakers, Droog Design/Spirit of the nineties, Amsterdam: 010, 1998.

Drutt, Helen and Peter Dormer, Jewelry of our time, New York: Thames & Hudson, 1995.

Elizabeth Callinicos

Born 1966, Wales, lives and works Great Haseley, Oxon, UK.

Elizabeth Callinicos began her training as a jeweller with a traditional apprenticeship in silver and goldsmithing in Athens and went onto receive her BA from West Surrey College of Art & Design and an MA from the Royal College of Art, London. Callinicos has had solo exhibitions throughout Europe and lectures regularly in colleges across the UK.

Selected Exhibitions

2004 Collect, The Victoria & Albert Museum, London

2000 Jerwood Applied Arts Prize, Crafts Council of England, London

1999 Elizabeth Callinicos, Galerie Sofie Lachaert, Belgium

Li-Sheng Cheng

Born 1970, Taipei, Taiwan, lives and works in London, UK.

Li-Sheng Cheng received her BA in jewellery design from Kent Institute of Art & Design in 2002 and her MA in Design from Sheffield Hallam University in 2004.

Selected Exhibitions

2004 New Designers, Business Desugn Centre, London

2003 Unusual Objects, The Craft Shop, Royal Exchange Theatre, Manchester
Valentines Exhibition, The Craft Centre, Leeds

Norman Cherry

Born 1949, lives and works in Birmingham, UK.

Dr Norman Cherry studied at Glasgow School of Art between 1966-1970 before becoming proprietor of the Woodmarket Gallery, Kelso, in 1971. Cherry has taught at various universities, and became Head of the School of Jewellery of the University of Central England in 1996. As well as designing jewellery, Cherry has written extensively on aspects of jewellery and body modification, with his current research being reflected in his Angiogenetic Body Adornment. He has won numerous awards including the Saltire Society John Noble Craft Award, and the Betty Davis Award for Jewellery.

Selected Exhibitions

2000 Norman Cherry, Hipotesi, Barcelona

1999 From the Center to the Edge, Institute of
      Contemporary Art, Portland, ME

1994 Norman Cherry, Scottish Gallery, Edinburgh

Colette Hazelwood

Born 1971, Manchester, UK where she lives and works.

Colette Hazelwood has been designing and making
contemporary jewellery for six years since graduating from
Manchester Metropolitan University in 1999 with a BA in
3D Design. She produces and sells her jewellery at the
Manchester Craft & Design Centre, lectures on jewellery
design in colleges around the UK, and has exhibited her
work internationally.

Selected Exhibitions

2003 Commission Me, Urbis, Manchester; Bluecoat,
      Liverpool, and Grundy Art Gallery, Blackpool

2002 Designing Ourselves, National Museum of
      Scotland, Edinburgh

2001 Make Me, Object Gallery, Sydney

Nanna Melland

Born 1969, Oslo, Norway, lives and works in Munich,
Germany.

In 1995 Nanna Melland began an apprenticeship in
goldsmithing, before studying at the Institute of Precious
Metals, Copenhagen, Denmark between 2000-2001.
Melland then went on to study at The Academy of Art
in Munich from 2001 to 2005, under the professorship
of Otto Künzli.

Selected Exhibitions

2004 Gallery Marzee, Nejimigen, Holland

2002 Gallery Oona, Berlin, Germany

2001 Gallery Aurum, Copenhagen, Denmark

Mike & Maaike

Maaike Evers was born 1971, Emmeloord, The
Netherlands. Mike Simonian was born 1971, Montebello,
CA, US. They live and work in San Francisco, CA.

Mike Simonian and Maaike Evers began collaborating on
product, furniture, and environmental design in 2000.

Evers received her BA from the Academy of Industrial
Design Eindhoven before moving to the US. Simonian
studied design at Art Center College of Design in
Pasadena, CA, and has since worked within numerous
furniture and industrial design companies. The pair's work
has been featured in numerous publications including
WIRED, Spin and Maxim, and has received several design
awards including ID Magazine Honorable Mention Awards
in 2004 and 2003.

Selected Exhibitions

2004 Thomas Heatherwick — Conran Foundation
      Collection, The Design Museum, London

2003 The Needs Trilogy: Act III — Healing, A benefit for
      Habitat for Humanity, San Francisco, CA
      Anti War Medals Show, Velvet Da Vinci,
      San Francisco, CA

Selected Publications

Pence, Angela, "Eclectica", San Francisco Chronicle, 1
January 2003.

Altman-Siegel, Vanessa, "Cross-purposes", Spin, November
2000, p. 90.

Spinrad, Paul, "Fetish", Wired, February 2000, p. 64.

Mah Rana

Born 1964, London, UK, where she lives and works.

Mah Rana has been making and exhibiting work for
nearly 20 years. She received her BA (Hons) Degree in
Silversmithing and Jewellery from Buckinghamshire
College in 1986 and and MA Degree in Jewellery from the
Royal College of Art, London, in 1989. Rana is currently
Programme Leader of 3D Design: Metalwork, Jewellery,
Glass and Ceramics at The Surrey Institute of Art and
Design. A concern for the personal and collective histories
and significance of jewellery pervades Mah Rana's oeuvre.

Selected Exhibitions

2004 Schmuck, Pinakothek der Moderne, Munich

2003 Inner Luxury, Fundació la Caixa, Barcelona

2002 Jewellery is Life, Fabrica Art Gallery, Brighton

Selected Publications

Rana, Mah, Jewellery is Life, Brighton: Fabrica, 2002.

Watkins, David, Design Source Book: Jewellery, London:
New Holland, 1999.

Game, Amanda, Jewellery Moves, Edinburgh, NMS
Publishing Ltd., 1998.

FASHION FORWARD

Solange Azagury-Partridge

Born 1961 in London, UK where she lives and works.

After studying Spanish and French in university, Solange Azagury-Partridge took a stopgap job with the costume jewellers Butler & Wilson and moved a year later to vintage jewellery dealer Gordon Watson. She began making jewellery for herself in 1987 and set up her own business three years later, quickly gaining acclaim for her iconoclastic approach to design. Azagury-Partridge worked as creative director for Boucheron Paris from 2001 to 2004 but left to concentrate on her own business. She has been nominated for the Design Museum's 2003 Designer of the Year award and has works in the permanent jewellery collection at the Musée des Artes Decoratifs du Louvre.

Lara Bohinc

Born 1972 in Slovenia, lives and works in London.

Bohinc first studied industrial design at the Ljubljana Academy of Fine Arts and later came to London where in 1996 she completed her MA in Jewellery and Metalwork at the Royal College of Art. She debuted at the London Fashion Week in 1997 and, along with winning the Marks and Spencers-sponsored New Generation Design Award, she established a reputation as a cutting-edge designer with both an architectural understanding and a feminine aesthetic. She has collaborated with a number of fashion designers, providing jewellery to complement their runway collections, and currently works as a freelance consultant for Cartier International.

Runway Collaborations

Costume National, Gucci, Lanvin, Exte, Guy Laroche, Christophe Lemaire, Uniforme

Erickson Beamon

Vicki Bea Sarge lives and works in London and Karen Erickson lives and works in New York.

Vicki Bea Sarge and Karen Erickson began collaborating as hometown friends in Detroit, Michigan, but moved to New York City in the early 1980s to bring their fashion designs to the runway. Moving quickly from clothing to accessory collections, the designers gained recognition and success and expanded into various retail outlets. In the past 20 years they've collaborated with dozens of major designers, securing themselves as much a place in haute couture as in street fashion. Having expanded into the London fashion market in 1985, Erickson Beamon continues to expand its collections of glamorous adornments around the globe.

Runway Collaborations

Alexander McQueen, Christian Dior, Givenchy, Imitation of Christ, John Galliano, Marc Jacobs, Oscar de la Renta

Selected Publications

2004   Harper's & Queen, March
        Vogue (Italia)
        Vogue (UK), July

Elizabeth Galton

Born 1976 in Wimbledon, UK, lives and works in Middlesex, UK.

Elizabeth Galton studied Design, Textile and Theatre Arts at the London College of Fashion, received her BA in Jewellery Design from Central Saint Martins in 1998, and her MA in Goldsmithing, Silversmithing, Metalwork and Jewellery from the Royal College of Art in 2000. Combining jewellery and sculpture in her oversized and opulent orchids, Galton brings cutting-edge technology to couture exhibitions throughout Europe and the US. Among her formal recognitions are the 2004 Craftsmanship & Design Award (GOLD) from Goldsmith's Design Council and the Craft Council's 2003 Development Award. She continues to inspire as a designer as well as a guest lecturer at the Royal College of Art.

Selected Exhibitions

2005   Collect, Victoria & Albert Museum represented by Lesley Crazy Gallery, London

2004   Runway Rocks Fashion Show by Swarovski, New York Fashion Week, NY
        Looking: Over My Shoulder, Lesley Craze Gallery, London

Shaun Leane

Born 1969, London, UK, where he lives and works.

Shaun Leane began his career in 1985 at age 16 with an apprenticeship in goldsmithing at English Traditional Jewellery in Hatton Garden, London, where he continued crafting delicate antique pieces until 1998. In 1991 he received Advanced Level City and Guilds in Fine Jewellery and Design Sir John Cass College, and began his collaborations with Alexander McQueen. While at English Traditional Jewellery, Leane also produced for Van Cleef &

Arpels, Garrads, Kutchinskys, and Mappin & Webb, and has been honoured as both recipient of and judge for numerous awards in jewellery design.

Runway Collaborations

Alexander McQueen, Givenchy, Swarovski

Selected Exhibitions

2004 Runway Rocks Fashion Show by Swarovski, New York Fashion Week, NY

2001 Fashion in Motion, The Victoria & Albert Muesum, London

1999 Violently Elegant (solo exhibition), Aurum Contemporary Jewellery Gallery, London

Daisuke Sakaguchi

Born 1981 in London, UK where he lives and works.

Daisuke Sakaguchi graduated from Central Saint Martins with an BA (Hons) in Jewellery Design and has since exhibited at the 2003 New Designers exhibition, 27 Degrees, Sian Evans Studio, and The British Arts Metal Society, where he received an Honorary Mention Award. Following the investment of Godrich DC in 2004, Sakaguchi completed several high profile commissions and recently launched his first collection through Comme des Garçons store in London. He continues to pursue his jewellery designs as well as exploring other areas of fashion and design, and is regularly called upon to design and create graffiti murals throughout the UK and Europe.

Selected Exhibitions

2003 New Designers Exhibition, London
Sian Evans Studio Exhibition, Clerkenwell, London

2001 British Arts Medal Society Exhibition, Window Gallery, Canary Wharf, London

Selected Publications

Observer Magazine, August 2004

Arena Homme Plus, Autumn/Winter 2003/2004

The Face, September 2003

Wouters & Hendrix

Katrin Wouters and Karen Hendrix live and work in Antwerp, Belgium.

In 1984, the design duo Katrin Wouters and Karen Hendrix graduated together from the Royal Academy of Fine Arts in Antwerp, having studied Goldsmithing. Their aspiration was to produce fine jewellery that is elegant and daring, intelligent and bold, exclusive and affordable. 20 years and no less than 40 diverse collections later, the best friends continue to progress and reinvent with new shapes and styles. Wouters & Hendrix opened their first flagship store in Antwerp in 2001 as their clientele continues to expand. Their mixed aesthetic of refinement, adventure, and humour has drawn collaboration with Dries Van Noten, Walter Van Beirendonck, Dirk Bikkembergs, Ann Demeulemeester, and Paul Smith.

TACTILE SCULPTURE

Anna Osmer Andersen

Born 1975, Denmark, lives and works in London, UK.

Anna Osmer Andersen is a Danish artist who moved to London in 1997 to start a jewellery course in traditional jewellery techniques. After graduating from London Guildhall University in 2001, she went on to exhibit her Poor but Posh collection in various galleries. In 2004 she completed her MA in Jewellery Design at the Royal College of Art and since then has shown her Chains & Pearls collection at the fashion boutique 'b-store', resulting in considerable press coverage, and the purchase of her works by the singer Bjork. Anna is currently working on a collection of smaller scale pieces with similar qualities to her earlier collection but more accessible.

Selected Exhibitions

2004   Degree Show, Gallerie Marzee, Netherlands. Crafts Council shop summer show, Victoria & Albert Museum, London

2003   SOFA Chicago, Crafts Council Gallery shop, London

Kristina Apostolou

Born 1982, Cyprus, Greece, lives and works in London, UK.

Kristina Apostolou graduated from Central St. Martins College of Art & Design in 2004. In her time at Central St. Martins she was recognised by Cool Diamonds and Cartier. Apostolou's work has been showcased around the world, most recently in an exhibition in Hong Kong held by the British Council.

Selected Exhibitions

2004   New Designers, Business Design Centre, London

2003   Inorghenta International Trade show, Munich

2002   Hidden Talents, EC One, London

Tomasz Donocik

Born 1981, Krakow, Poland, lives and works in London, UK.

Tomasz Donocik received his BA (Hons) in Jewellery Design from Central St Martins College of Art & Design in 2004 and is currently pursuing an MA in Goldsmithing, Silversmithing, Metalwork and Jewellery design at the Royal College of Art, London. He has exhibited his jewellery in galleries throughout Europe and has won the Ebel Haute Couture watch project, involving Scholarship at the Ebel Headquarters.

Selected Exhibitions

2004   Directions, Lethaby Gallery, Central St. Martins College, London

2002   Hidden Talents, EC One, London

2003   Inorghenta International Trade show, Munich

Arline Fisch

Born 1931, New York, NY, US, lives and works in San Diego, CA, US.

Arline Fisch has played a central role in the revitalisation of jewellery as a contemporary art form. Her outstanding contribution has been the introduction of weaving techniques into the field of jewellery making. In 1985, Fisch was declared a "Living Treasure of California" by the State Assembly for her work as an artist, educator and author. Having founded the Jewellery and Metalsmithing programme at San Diego State University in 1961 and taught there for over 30 years, Arline Fisch has obtained the prestigious role of Professor Emeritus of Art. She is Director and Vice President of the World Crafts Council and serves as Trustee of the American Craft Council. Originally from Brooklyn, New York, Fisch received degrees from Skidmore College and the University of Illinois. She is the recipient of two Fulbright Scholarships to attend the School of Arts and Crafts in Copenhagen and to pursue independent research. Her work is represented in numerous collections including the Vatican Museum in Rome, The Victoria & Albert Museum in London and the Museum of Arts and Design in New York.

Selected Exhibitions

2000–2002 Elegant Fantasy: The Jewellery of Arline Fisch, Oakland Museum, CA; Textile Museum, Washington DC; American Craft Museum, NY

1997   Celebrating American Craft 1975–1995, Danish Museum of Decorative Art, Copenhagen

1992   American Crafts: The Nation's Collection, Renwick Gallery, Washington DC

Selected Publications

Fisch, Arlene, Textile Techniques in Metal [1975], New York: Lark, 2001.

Danielle Gordon

Born 1983, lives and works in Glasgow, Scotland.

Danielle Gordon graduated with a first class degree in Jewellery and Metal Design from Duncan of Jordonstone College of Art and Design, Dundee, Scotland, 2004. She was awarded a bursary in 2004 to undertake an internship in New York at the Museum of Modern Art, and is currently setting up a jewellery studio in Glasgow.

Selected Exhibitions

2005 National Trust for Scotland Craft Shops, Glasgow

2004 BraveArt, London
New Designers, London

Maria Hanson

Born 1967, lives and works in Sheffield, UK.

Maria Hanson received her BA (Hons) in Three-Dimensional Design from West Surrey College of Art and Design, Farnham, in 1989, after which she completed an MA in Goldsmithing, Silversmithing, Metalwork and Jewellery at the Royal College of Art, London in 1991. Since graduating she has taught at numerous colleges in the UK, she has recently become Course Director at the University of Central England's School of Jewellery. Her jewellery is represented in numerous collections including The Crafts Council Collection, London, and The National Museums of Scotland, Edinburgh.

Selected Exhibitions

2003-2004 CHESS, touring exhibition, Velvet da Vinci, San Francisco; Scotland; London; New Orleans

2000 Jerwood Jewellery Prize (Shortlist), Crafts Council, London

1998 Solo Exhibition, Jewellery Focus, Contemporary Applied Arts, London

Selected Publications

European Triennial of Contemporary Jewellery, 2002

From the Centre to the Edge, ICA: Portland, MA, 1999

Adele Kime

Born 1973, Stockport, Cheshire, lives and works in New Mills, Derbyshire, UK.

Since completing her degree in Design from Liverpool University in 2001, Adele had been working as a freelance jewellery designer. In 2002, Kime was awarded the

NextMove prize by the Crafts Council and she is currently a member of the Association for Contemporary Jewellers. Her work is sold in Liverpool and Leeds City Art Gallery. Until last year she has been Designer in Residence at Manchester Metropolitan University.

Selected Exhibitions

2004 Christmas Exhibition, Designer Jewellers Group, Barbican, London
Lesley Craze Gallery, London

2003 The Teapot Redefined, Mobilia Gallery, SOFA, Chicago

2001 New Designers, Business Design Centre, London

Daniela Schwartz

Born 1972, Buenos Aires, Argentina, lives and works in Strasbourg, France.

Daniela Schwartz studied for a BA in Fashion and Textile Design at the University of Buenos Aires between 1991 and 1994. Following this, Schwartz studied in a number of diverse disciplines, which have fed into her jewellery practice: tinwork, sculpture, costume design, theatrical make-up and dance. In 1998 she set up the Quarto contemporary jewellery label with Marina Mollinelli Wells, and pursued her jewellery design in tandem with her research and performance of improvisional dance. She has taught at a number of universities and 2004-2005 went to study jewellery design at the Ecole Superieure des Arts Decoratifs, Strasbourg, France.

Selected Exhibitions

2005 Forvm Gallery, Barcelona, Spain

2004 Metallisteria, Contemporary Jewellery Gallery, Buenos Aires, Argentina

2003 Jess James Gallery, London

Selected Publications

Elle, Buenos Aires, February 2003.

FASE, magazine of experimental design, Buenos Aires, November 2002.

La Nacion, special issue on contemporary jewellery, Buenos Aires, November 2000.

Vannetta Seecharran

Born 1969, Guyana, South America, lives and works in London, UK.

Having completed a BA in Product Design and Jewellery from Parsons School of Design in New York and a MA in Jewellery from the State University of New York, Vannetta Seecharran has been exhibiting internationally and working as a freelance designer. She has been awarded grants from both the Crafts Council and Arts Council, London. Seecharran's work is held in the permanent collection at the Montreal Museum of Decorative Arts in Canada.

Selected Exhibitions

2004 Feast your Eyes, Crafts Council at the Victoria & Albert Museum, London

2003 J+T Jewellery Meets Textiles, Contemporary Applied Arts, London

2000 British Design, Chic Choc, Germany

Sissi Westerberg

Born 1975, Stockholm, lives and works in Stockholm, Sweden.

Sissi Westerberg has been exhibiting internationally since her BA in Metal Craft and Jewellery from Konstfack University College of Arts, Craft and Design, Stockholm, Sweden, where she also recently completed her MA. Westerberg has been involved with curating exhibitions, seminars and workshops in her home city.

Selected Exhibitions

2004 Nordic Cool — Hot Women Designers, National Museum of Women in Arts, Washington DC Designed Sweden, Museum of London, Museum in Docklands; Pacific Design Center, Los Angeles

2001 Design Objects 2001, On Sundays, Tokyo

Christoph Zellweger

Born in 1962 in Lubeck, Germany, lives in Sheffield, UK.

Christoph Zellweger received his Goldsmith Certificate through apprenticeship in Lubeck and Kiel from 1980 to 1984, and while working as a professional goldsmith in the 1980s and early 1990s he studied Sculpture at Kunstegewerbeschule Zurich. In 1993, he received his MA with Distinction from the Royal College of Art in London, and he has since worked as professor and lecturer in Metalwork, Jewellery and Industrial Design while also pursuing freelance design and various experimental projects. His work has seen acclaim in Germany, Sweden, Switzerland, Belgium, Austria, England, and Portugal, and he continues to exhibit and create throughout Europe.

Selected Exhibitions

2004 Meeting Points, Foundation Bulbenkian, Lisbon, Portugal

2003 World Craft Forum Invitational, Kanzawa, Japan Fremd-Kurper, solo exhibition, Galerie Tactile, Geneva, Switzerland

NEW GEOMETRIES

Elizabeth Bone

Born 1964, Nottingham, UK, lives and works in London, UK.

Having completed a Foundation Course in Art and Design at Trent Polytechnic in Nottingham, Elizabeth Bone went on to earn her BA in Crafts Combined Studies (wood, metal, ceramics, textiles) at Crewe and Alsager College in 1988 and establish her own studio workshop in 1991. She received her Teachers Certificate in 1993, and has since lectured and tutored part time in Jewellery and Silversmithing at West Hertfordshire College, University of Derby, and Manchester Metropolitan University. Her work has been widely exhibited and published in galleries and design sourcebooks throughout Europe and the US.

Selected Exhibitions

2004–2005 200 Rings, Velvet da Vinci, San Francisco, Tuscon, Maine, US

2004   Looking: Over My Shoulder, Lesley Craze Gallery, London

2000   SOFA (International Exhibition of Sculpture Objects & Functional Art), Chicago, IL

Selected Publications

Le Van, Marthe ed., 1000 Rings, North Carolina: Lark Books, 2004.

Oliver, Elizabeth, The Art of Jewellery Design, London: Quarto Publishing, 2002.

Metalsmith: Exhibition in Print, Naperville: Society of North American Goldsmiths, 2000.

Gill Forsbrook

Born 1961, Birmingham, UK, lives and works in Cambridgeshire, UK.

Gill Forsbrook graduated from Manchester Polytechnic in 1982 with a BA (Hons) in Three Dimensional Design with specialisation in metalwork and jewellery. After pursuing work in other areas, she established her own business as a design maker in 1997 and has since exhibited and sold her jewellery through galleries in the UK and abroad. Known for her emphasis on a variety of plastics, Gill avidly explores their unique properties — translucency, transparency, flexibility, and freedom of colour. Typically working in small batch production, Gill is continuing to create and develop her designs whilst seeking opportunities to further exhibit her work.

Selected Exhibitions

2004   Looking: Over My Shoulder, Lesley Craze Gallery, London
       Dazzle, Princes Square, Glasgow;
       National Theatre, London

2003   Jewelry Hard and Soft, The Society of Arts and Crafts, Boston, MA

Laura Gates

Born 1976, lives and works in Brighton, UK.

After Laura Gates earned her BA (Hons) in Silversmithing and Jewellery at London Guildhall University in 1998 she established her own business in London as jewellery designer in 1999 and moved her studio to Brighton in 2002. She has received awards in both jewellery design and management and continues to pursue and exhibit her works — which include jewellery and wall designs — throughout the UK.

Selected Exhibitions

2004   Select: Covetable Contemporary Crafts, Yorkshire Craft Centre, Bradford
       Showcase, Mead Gallery, Warwick Arts Centre, Warwick

2003   Chelsea Craft Fair 2003, Chelsea Town Hall, London

Selected Publications

Crafts magazine, May–June 2003.

"Focus on London", Breeze, Japan, February 2002.

Bard, Elizabeth, "Redefining the Jewel", Art Review, January 2002.

Marina Molinelli Wells

Born 1972, Buenos Aires, Argentina, where she lives and works.

Marina Molinelli Wells received a degree in Industrial Design from the University of Buenos Aires in 1999, but she began studying contemporary jewellery with Jorge Castañon at his studio La Nave in 1994. Her post-graduate university work includes courses in business and design and metalwork, but she has also studied art and dance history, glass modelling and painting and special effects, masks, and artistic makeup. In June 2004, she and designer Francisca Kweitel launched Metalisteria, a new exhibition space for contemporary jewellery. Known for her dramatic combination of natural and industrial elements, Molinelli Well's jewellery reflects her diverse studies and her commitment to a continued discovery and development.

Selected Exhibitions

2004   Fashion Week, Buenos Aires
         Joyas, Joias, Latin American Artists,
         Velvet da Vinci Gallery, San Francisco, CA
         Premiere Classe Fashion Trade Show, Paris

Selected Publications

A Look in Contemporary Jewellery, Buenos Aires: Centro Cultural Recoleta, 2003.

"Joias", Vogue Brasil, 2003.

Kamilla Ruberg

Born 1975, Copenhagen, Denmark, lives and works in London, UK.

Kamilla Ruberg has studied extensively in silversmithing, goldsmithing, metalwork and jewellery design, having completed her BA (Hons) at London Guildhall University in 1999, and her MA at London's Royal College of Art in 2002. Her modern and innovative jewellery has received awards from various craft councils including the Copenhagen Goldsmiths Guild, Crafts Council, UK, and the World Gold Council, and her distinctive kinetic pieces have recently been purchased for collection by the Danish Art Foundation and the Contemporary Art Society, UK. Ruberg continues to create new pieces from her studio store in Islington, London and exhibits her work in a variety of contemporary spaces.

Selected Exhibitions

2005   Collect, Victoria & Albert Museum represented
         by Lesley Crazy Gallery, London

2004   Rings-Symbols-Inspiration, The National
         Museum, Copenhagen

2004   Solo exhibition, Copenhagen Goldsmiths
         Guild, Copenhagen

Selected Publications

Ringe I Dialog, Copenhagen: Kjóbenhavns Guldsmedelaug, 2004

TELLING STORIES

Vicki Ambery-Smith

Born 1950, Leeds, lives and works in London, UK.

After studying at Middlesex Polytechnic and Gmund Fachnochscule, Schwabisch, Vicki Ambery-Smith set up her studio in 1977 with the aid of a Crafts Council grant. Since, she has exhibited throughout the UK and internationally, in Europe, the US and Japan. Ambery-Smith has carried out commissions for the Crafts Council and having become known for her miniature architecturally inspired pieces, was asked by the late Sam Wanamaker to make work for the Shakespeare Globe Project, including a model of the theatre itself to be presented to Prince Philip. Her work is in the permanent collections of the Victoria & Albert Museum, London and the Royal Museum of Scotland.

Selected Exhibitions

2004 Collect, Victoria & Albert Museum, London

2000 The Scottish Gallery, Edinburgh (solo exhibition)

1998 Introducing Contemporary British Jewellery, Society of Arts and Crafts, Boston

Selected Publications

O'Day, Deirdre, "The Architectural Portraits of Vicki Ambery-Smith", Metalsmith, vol. 25, 2005.

Turner, Ralph, review of exhibition at Rutford Craft Centre, Crafts, January/February 1992.

Watkins, David, Design Source Book: Jewellery, London: New Holland, 1999.

Jivan Astfalck

Born in Berlin, Germany, lives and works in London, UK.

Having trained in the German apprenticeship system to qualify and work as a goldsmith in Berlin, Jivan Astfalck moved to London in 1985 where she established her self-employed practice making jewellery for sale and commissions, and conceptual work. She has also continued to write, research and teach whilst in the UK, receiving her MA in the History and Theory of Modern Art and undertaking doctoral research at Chelsea College of Art and Design. In 2004, Astfalck was given the post of Senior Research Fellow in the School of Jewellery at the Birmingham Institute of Art and Design (University of Central England) where she is now also course director of the MA in Jewellery and Silversmithing and Related

Products. She has contributed to various conferences, symposia and publications, and has had her work exhibited internationally.

Selected Exhibitions

2005 SELF, Angel Row Gallery, Nottingham; Bury St Edmunds Art Gallery; mac, Birmingham

2004 The Stuff of Life, Visual Research Centre, Dundee Contemporary Arts
Dust to Dust, University Gallery, University of Essex

Selected Writing

Crafts in Dialogue: Six Views on a Practice in Change, Sweden: Craft in Dialogue/IASPIS publication, 2005

"Beyond Adornment", catalogue essay for Beyond Adornment, Sweden, 2003

"Skin-Carnival", in Nocturnus, Muhu Island/Tallinn, Estonia, 2001

Jo Bagshaw

Born 1967, Altrincham, Cheshire, UK, lives and works in York, UK.

Having received her BA in Metalwork and Jewellery from Sheffield Hallam University in 2004, Jo Bagshaw is currently studying on the Visual Enterprise Course at York College. Whilst on the course she has been commissioned to design and make a 'crown' for the Miss York competition and has been collaborating with fashion students developing a collection of body adornment around the theme of recycling and re-use.

Selected Exhibitions

2004 New Designers, Business Design Centre, London

2002 Cupola Gallery, Sheffield
Pomp and Circumstance, York City Art Gallery

Tomoko Hayashi

Born 1980, Hyogo, Japan, lives and works in London, UK.

Whilst completing her BA in Fine Art at Kyota Seika University, Japan, Tomoko Hayashi began to focus on an exploration of human skin, leading her to study the MA course in Design for Textiles Futures at Central Saint Martins, London between 2002 and 2004. As a result, her conceptual practice is a unique blend of installation, textiles and jewellery, an approach that she has further diversified by undertaking research as an intern at Media

Lab Europe, during 2004, where she has developed an interactive 'communication environment' for long-distance partners.

Selected Exhibitions

2005 Touch Me, Victoria & Albert Museum, London

2004-2005 Direction, Lethaby Gallery, London

Alyssa Dee Krauss

Born 1962, Hempstead, NY, US, lives and works in Leeds, MA, US.

Since receiving her MFA from the Rhode Island School of Design, Alyssa Dee Krauss has been working to create jewellery as a fine art form. Throughout 1996 and 1997 she taught as Professor of Jewellery and Metals at Savannah College of Art and Design and in 2003 sat on the Board of Directors of the Northampton Council of Arts in 2003. Dee Krauss has been awarded an artist fellowship from the National Endowment for the Arts, and in 1998 she received the Claude Monet Foundation Artist Residency Grant. Her work is in the permanent collections of the Museum of Contemporary Arts in New York and the Montreal Museum of Art.

Selected Exhibitions

2003 Corporal Identity: Body Language: 9th Triennial for Form and Content, Museum für Angewandte Kunst, Frankfurt; Klingspor-Museum, Offenbach, Germany; Museum of Arts & Design, New York

2000 Wearable Sculpture, Montreal Museum of Fine Arts, Montreal

1999 Metalanguage (solo exhibition), Barbican Centre, London

Selected Publications

"Alyssa Dee Krauss: Bindings", Metalsmith Magazine, Spring 2003.

Le Monde, 3 June 1999.

Vogue, Paris, March 1999.

Francisca Kweitel

Born 1974, Buenos Aires, Argentina, where she lives and works.

Having studied jewellery with the noted Catalan jeweller, Ramon Puig Cuyas, as well as sculpture at the Massana School in Barcelona, and a course in fashion design, in 2003 Francisca Kweitel was awarded a scholarship from

Argentina's Secretary for Culture. She is a founding member of "Peu de Reina", an artistic jewellery association inaugurated in 2001 that exhibits throughout Spain and South America, and has organised and contributed to conferences on the subject of contemporary jewellery. In 2004 she opened "Metalisteria", a contemporary jewellery shop in her native Buenos Aires. Kweitel has been chosen to participate in Talente 2005, an international competition for young makers in crafts, design and technology that takes place in Munich each year.

Selected Exhibitions

2004 Joyas, Joias, Latin American Artists, Velvet da Vinci Gallery, San Francisco, CA

2003-2004 Anti War Medals, Velvet Da Vinci Gallery, San Francisco, CA; Victoria & Albert Museum, London, FAD, Barcelona

2003 Silver Schools, touring throughout Poland

Hannah Louise Lamb

Born 1977, St Austell, UK, where she lives and works.

Since receiving her BA in Silversmithing and Jewellery from Glasgow School of Art in 2000 and her MA in Goldsmithing, Silversmithing, Metalwork and Jewellery from the Royal College of Art, London in 2004, Hannah Louise Lamb has worked as a freelance jewellery designer and maker, exhibiting throughout the UK and producing commissioned work. She has also assisted in teaching at Edinburgh College of Art and at the Kaarukal Foundation in New Delhi. In 2004 the Scottish Arts Council awarded Lamb a set-up grant.

Selected Exhibitions

2005 Contemporary Jewellery from Britain, Bielak Gallery, Poland

2004-2005 Dazzle, Princes Square, Glasgow; National Theatre, London

2004 Designer Jewellers Group, Barbican Centre, London

Laura Potter

Born 1971, Stourbridge, UK, lives and works in London, UK.

Since receiving her BA in Silversmithing and Jewellery from the University of Central England and her MA in Goldsmithing, Silversmithing, Metalwork and Jewellery from the Royal College of Art, Laura Potter has remained in London, producing jewellery for exhibitions and commissions. She has also been involved in projects that aim to widen people's access to, and understanding of, contemporary craft practices. Since 1998, Potter has taught on the undergraduate design programme at Goldsmiths College, London. Her work is in the collections of National Museums of Scotland, the Crafts Council and the British Council, London.

Selected Exhibitions

2004 What is Craft?, The Hub, Lincolnshire
      Treasure, The Pearoom Centre, Lincolnshire

2002 Commissioning and Community, The Cleveland
      Craft Centre, Middlesborough

1999 Metalmorphosis, British Council Touring
      Exhibition, Hungary/Germany

Hans Stofer

Born 1957, Baden, Switzerland, lives and works in London, UK.

After training as a precision engineer and toolmaker, Hans Stofer completed his MA in Jewellery and Design at Zurich School of Art in 1984. He now works not only as a designer and maker, but as a teacher, writer, curator and in his own words, an "ambassador for promoting the handmade, designed object with meaning". Stofer is currently Subject Leader for Silversmithing and Metalwork at Camberwell College of Art (University of the Arts, London) and Associate Lecturer on the MA Applied Design course at the Sandberg Institute, Amsterdam. He also advises on design methodology at London Metropolitan University. His own work is shown internationally and is in the permanent collections of Danner Stiftung and Pinakothek der Moderne in Munich and the Crafts Council and the Contemporary Art Society in London.

Selected Exhibitions

2004 Collect, Victoria & Albert Museum, London

2003 Recycling Design, Musee de Design et d'Arts
      Appliques Contemporains, Lausanne

2002–2003 Micromegas, touring exhibition, Bayerischer
      Kunstgewerbe Galerie, Munich; American Craft
      Museum, New York, NY; Musée de l'horologerie
      et de l'émaillerie, Geneva; Gallery Yu, Tokyo;
      Power House Museum, Sydney

Selected Publications

Greenhalgh, Paul ed., The Persistence of Craft, London: A&C Black Publishers, 2002.

Peters, Tessa and Janice West eds, The Uncanny Room, London: Luminous Books, 2001.

Stofer, Hans, "Contemporary Crafts", Craft in Dialogue, IASPIS project publication, 2005.

COLOUR AND LIGHT

Harriet Clayton

Born 1979, lives and works in London, UK.

On graduating from Central St Martins in 2002 with a BA (Hons) in Jewellery Design, Harriet Clayton set up her studio in East London and has since designed and produced three seasonal collections. Her work is stocked by Harvey Nichols and Liberty in London, and held at various boutiques across the UK and abroad. She has also worked on private and press commissions, producing Swarovski-studded oversize visors and laser-engraved acrylic headpieces.

Selected Exhibitions

2004 London Fashion Week, Duke of York
Headquarters, London
New Designer Showcase, Platina, Stockholm

2003 Dazzle, Princes Square, Glasgow;
National Theatre, London

Selected Publications

Yvonne Kulagowski, The Earrings Book, London: A&C Black, 2005.

Sarah Crawford

Born 1970, Oxford, lives and works in London, UK.

Sarah Crawford trained in Jewellery Design at Middlesex University, obtaining her MA in 1995. She has held visiting and part time lectureships at Edinburgh College of Art, De Montford University, London Guildhall University, and a number of other institutions; she has also led various crafts workshops for children of all ages. Both private and public collections in the US and the UK hold pieces of her work, and she has made commissioned pieces for the Bowes Museum and the City Gallery in Leicester, amongst others. An active member of the jewellery-making community, she has organised seminars and discussions for the Association of Contemporary Jewellery and worked in various departments at the Crafts Council.

Selected Exhibitions

2003 Earring, Mobilia Gallery, Cambridge, MA

2002 Weaving Stories, Brochocka Baynes & City
Art Centre, Edinburgh
Echt Kunst Stoff, Galerie V&V, Vienna

Selected Publications

Hoggard, Liz, "New Commissions for Bankfield Museum", Crafts, January/February 2002.

Bard, Elizabeth, "Redefining the Jewel", Art Review, January 2002.

Nicolas Estrada

Born 1972, Medellin, Colombia, lives and works in Barcelona, Spain.

While studying for a MA in Marketing in Barcelona, having worked in business for six years, Nicolas Estrada chose a change of direction and enrolled at the Escuela Massana for an Artistic Jewellery course. He is currently studying sculpture at the same school, and also holds qualifications in engraving, gemology, and casting, all skills which feed in to his design practice. He has won several awards including First Prize at the Midora Fair, and was a finalist for the Swarovski prize in 2003.

Selected Exhibitions

2004 Joyas, Joias, Latin American Artists,
Velvet da Vinci Gallery, San Francisco, CA
Two Worlds, Galeria Magari, Barcelona

2003 Change Your Step, Galeria la Santa, Barcelona

Selected Publications

Jet Set Magazine, no. 61, 2003.

Contraste Newspaper, no. 52, 2003.

Melanie Hall

Born 1980, Torquay, Devon, UK, where she lives and works.

Melanie holds a National Diploma in Art and Design, and an FdA in Integrated Crafts from South Devon College, and has begun to garner notice for her colourful jewellery.

Selected Exhibitions

2004 New Designers, London

2003 The Spanish Barn, Torquay

Sarah King

Born 1965 Sussex, UK, lives and works in London, UK.

Since graduating in Fine Art from Goldsmith's College, University of London in 1987, Sarah King has been designing and making jewellery in London. In 1995, King was the recipient of The London Arts Board Award to an Individual Artist. She has exhibited internationally and is also in the collection of Museum für Kunst and Gewerbe, Hamburg. Her first collection was bought by Barneys, New York in 1992. The production range is sold internationally such as in Crafts Council at the Victoria & Albert Museum, Liberty and Conran, all London, Hilde Leiss, Hamburg and Kath Libbert, Bradford.

Selected Exhibitions

2003   Looking: over my Shoulder, Lesley Craze
       Gallery, London
       Sarah King Light Constructions, (solo exhibition),
       Arai Atelier Gallery, Tokyo

2001   Summer Showcase, Crafts Council at Victoria &
       Albert Museum, London

Selected Publications

Van Niftik, Syann, Jewellery using Natural Materials, 2005.

W Magazine, custom made wood pieces for Kate Moss, May 2004.

Sarah Lindsay

Born 1978, lives and works in London, UK.

Having obtained a first class degree in Silversmithing and Jewellery from Glasgow School of Art, Sarah Lindsay went on to complete a MA in Applied Arts Jewellery at the Royal College of Art in 2002. She has exhibited around the UK, and won the Cockpit Arts Seedbed Award in 2002. In the same year, she was shortlisted for the Stella McCartney competition.

Selected Exhibitions

2005   Handmade Plastics, The Craft and Design
       Gallery, Leeds

2004   Dazzle, Manchester Town Hall

2003   One Year On: New Designers, Islington
       Design Centre, London

Marlene McKibbin

Born 1953, Newry, County Down, Northern Ireland, lives and works in London, UK.

Marlene McKibbin has been making jewellery for over 20 years, having graduated from the Royal College of Art with a MA in Design in 1978. She has been a pioneer in the field of design-oriented jewellery, with collections of her work for public display housed in a number of museums in England and Scotland. She has exhibited all over Europe, and in Tokyo, Brisbane, and New York. Her work is informed by a minimalist aesthetic, and she is known for her attention to simple form.

Selected Exhibitions

2002   Triennale Europeenne du Bijou Contemporain,
       Seneffe, Belgium

2001   Jewellery by the Top Ten, Contemporary
       Applied Arts, London

1999   Stigma, Bluecoat Display Centre, Liverpool

Selected Publications

Katz, Sylvia, Classic Plastics: From Bakelite to High-tech, with a Collector's Guide, London: Thames & Hudson, 1985.

Tom Mehew

Born 1979, lives and works in London, UK.

Tom graduated from the BA in Jewellery Design at Central St Martins in 2001; the college bought four pieces from his degree show to add to their collection. Describing himself as a "three-dimensional designer", he has extended the methods he started using as a jeweller to create lighting and interior products. He has exhibited internationally, and won the first prize for Design at the Talente exhibition at the Munich Trade Fair in 2003. Stockists of his work include Lesley Craze in Clerkenwell, London, and the Gallerie Biro, Munich.

Selected Exhibitions

2003   Jewellery: New Alternatives, Glynn Vivian
       Art Gallery, Swansea
       Talente, Munich
       Waste to Taste, Sothebys, London

Selected Publications

Turner, Ralph, "Just the Ticket", Crafts magazine, September/October 2002.

Kathie Murphy

Born 1966, Meknes, Morocco, lives and works in London, UK.

Having obtained a BA (Hons) from Middlesex Polytechnic in 1990, Kathie Murphy went on to study at the Glasgow School of Art, completing her Post Graduate Diploma in 1992. In 1990, she was awarded an Equipment and Setting Up Grant by the Princes Youth Business Trust; she is on the Crafts Council index of selected makers, and is a part of the organisation and management team behind the London Dazzle exhibitions. Her work is held in collections in the National Museum of Scotland in Edinburgh, the Aberdeen City Art Gallery, and the Cleveland International Jewellery Collection.

Selected Exhibitions

2004 Jewellery Unlimited, Bristol

2003 Kathie Murphy (solo exhibition),
      Scottish Gallery, Edinburgh

2002 European Contemporary Jewellery Triennial
      Exhibition, World Crafts Council, Belgium

Adam Paxon

Born 1972, Penrith, Cumbria, UK, lives and works in Glasgow, Scotland.

Adam Paxon trained at Middlesex University, where he obtained a first class degree in Jewellery in 1995; he went on to attend the Onno Boekhouldt Masterclass at Edinburgh College of Art in 1998. He has exhibited widely and won the Herbert Hofmann Prize in 2002. Aside from his teaching position at Glasgow School of Art, he has been a visiting lecturer at the University of Ulster, the University of Central England, and a number of other institutions. His workshops centre upon the inventive use of plastic materials that his own work is known for.

Selected Exhibitions

2004 Collect, Victoria & Albert Museum, London

2003 anima, Scottish Gallery, Edinburgh

2001 Adam Paxon, Galleri Hnoss, Gothenburg, Sweden

Selected Publications

Ebendorf, Robert W ed., 1000 Rings, New York: Lark Books, 2004.

Kulagowski, Yvonne, The Earrings Book, London: A&C Black, 2005.

Zobel-Biro, Olga, Plastic Jewellery Art, Stuttgart: Arnoldsche Art Publishers, 2005.

Kaz Robertson

Lives and works in Edinburgh, Scotland.

Kaz Robertson holds a first class BA (Hons) and a Post Graduate Diploma in Jewellery from Edinburgh College of Art. Since graduating in 2002 she has set up the Diverse Workshop with Sally Moore and Donna Barry, based at the Coburg Studios in Edinburgh. She has exhibited widely, been recommended by The List, was awarded the Deutsche Bank Pyramid Award in 2002 and was shortlisted for the Janet Fitch Award for Jewellery in October 2003.

Selected Exhibitions

2004 Showcase, The Lighthouse, Glasgow
      SOFA NY, Mobilia Gallery, Cambridge, MA

2003 Spotlight Exhibition, Lesley Craze Gallery, London

Anoush Waddington

Born 1962 Sao Paolo, Brazil, lives and works in High Wycombe, Buckinghamshire.

Since graduating from the London School of Gemstone Cutting and Design, Anoush Waddington has been designing jewellery and working in areas including interior design and millinery and has exhibited extensively in Britain. She is currently Vice Chairman of the Designer Jewellers Group and has presented a contemporary jewellery workshop at the Victoria & Albert Museum. Outlets and exhibitions include Lesley Craze, the Victoria & Albert Museum and Electrum, all London; Facets Gallery, Devon; Habitat, Prague and OXOXO, Maryland, US.

Selected Exhibitions

2002 Society of Designer Crafts, The Mall Gallery

2004 Collect, Victoria & Albert Museum, London

2001 World Competition of Arts & Crafts,
      Kanazawa, Japan

DECORATIVE ELEMENTS

Kathleen Bailey

Lives and works in London, UK.

Since graduating from London Guildhall University with a BA in Silversmithing Jewellery and Allied Crafts, Kathleen Bailey has set up a business from her studio at Cockpit Arts. In the three years since graduating she has won a number of awards, including the Cockpit Arts Seedbed Award in June of 2004, and the Crafts Council Development Award. Her work has been shown in a number of galleries around the UK and Europe, and is held at the Scottish Gallery, the Hub in Edinburgh, and in galleries in Germany and Norway. Features in Vogue, FT Weekend, Elle and Crafts magazines, among others, have also shown her jewellery, and in 2004 she worked on a photo shoot for Greek Vogue with David Bailey.

Selected Exhibitions

2002–2004 Moving Dialogue, London, Florence and Inhorgenta, Munich

2004   Jewellery Unlimited, Bristol City Museum and Art Gallery

2003   thecentralhouse Christmas Show, thecentralhouse, London

Selected Publications

Ebendorf, Robert W ed., 1000 Rings, New York: Lark Books, 2004.

Donna Barry

Lives and works in Edinburgh, Scotland.

In 2002, having studied Jewellery and Silversmithing to postgraduate level at the Edinburgh College of Art, Donna Barry helped set up the Diverse Workshop studio in Edinburgh with the aid of a Deutsche Bank business start up grant. She has won awards and commendations at the Goldsmiths Company awards, and exhibited around Scotland, England, Wales, and the United States. Her jewellery is stocked in a number of outlets, including the Crafts Council Shop at the Victoria & Albert Museum, London.

Selected Exhibitions

2004   Dazzle, Traverse Theatre, Edinburgh
       New Faces, Victoria & Albert Museum Shop, London

2003   Botanical Jewellery, Mobilia Gallery, Boston, MA

Peter Chang

Born 1944, London, UK, lives and works in Glasgow, Scotland.

Having completed his Foundation year at Liverpool College of Art in 1963, Chang went on to obtain qualifications in Printmaking and Sculpture from Atelier 17 in Paris and the Slade School of Art, London. He has had a varied and prolific career, his work having been exhibited widely and held in public collections all over Europe and the United States; he has been commissioned by the World Gold Council in Paris, the Louis Koch collection in Switzerland, the Missoni collection in Milan, the British Council, and countless other public and private clients. He has been winning awards for his distinctive work with objects since the beginning of his career in the 1960s, including most recently the Herbert Hofmann Preis in 2003.

Selected Exhibitions

2005   Plastica, Soggotto del Desiderio, Palazzo Ducale, Mantua, Italy

2004   Collect, International Art Fair, Victoria & Albert Museum, London

2002–2003 Peter Chang: It's Only Plastic..., touring Germany

Selected Publications

Holzach, Cornelie, Peter Chang: Jewellery, Objects, Sculptures, Stuttgart: Arnoldsche, 2002.

Phillips, Clare, Jewels and Jewellery, London: Victoria & Albert Publications, 2000.

Watkins, David, Design Source Book: Jewellery, London: New Holland, 1999.

Gerda Flöckinger

Born 1927, Innsbruck, Austria, lives and works in London, UK.

Gerda Flöckinger has been among the most influential figures in British design over the last half century. She started out, having studied at St Martin's College and the Central School in London, exhibiting at the ICA and alongside her mother's fashion collections; from 1956 to 1960 Mary Quant and Alexander Plunkett Greene showed her work in the first Bazaar in the King's Road, London. She was the first living woman to be invited to have a solo show at the Victoria & Albert Museum and in the late 1960s, together with a group of other makers, was instrumental in the formation of the Crafts Advisory Council, now the Crafts Council, as well as setting up the first course on experimental jewellery design. She was awarded the CBE in 1991, was included in Who's Who in 2004, and continues to design and make jewellery both for galleries and private commission.

Selected Exhibitions

1961 Goldsmiths' Hall International Exhibition, London

1971 and 1986 Solo exhibitions, Victoria & Albert Museum, London

2001 The Ring, Mobilia Gallery, Cambridge, MA

Selected Publications

Phillips, Clare, Jewels and Jewellery, London: Victoria & Albert Publications, 2000

Harrod, Tanya, Crafts in Britain in the Twentieth Century, New Haven, CT: Yale University Press, 1999

de Cerval, Marguerite, Dictionnaire International du Bijou, Paris: Editions du Regard, 1998

Harrod, Tanya, essay on Flöckinger in Pioneers of Modern Craft, Margot Coatts ed., Manchester: Manchester University Press, 1997

Anna Lewis

Born 1976, Wales, lives and works in Swansea, Wales.

Anna Lewis was awarded a setting up grant in 2001 from The Crafts Council and Arts Council of Wales, after she graduated with a BA (Hons) in Jewellery from Middlesex University in 2000. Since then, her work has been featured in a number of high profile magazines including Elle Decoration, Living Etc., and Wedding and Home; model Elle McPherson has bought her work, and she has exhibited in Europe, Kuwait, the US and Australia. She has run children's workshops in Kuwait, and held a number of teaching and Artist in Residence positions around Wales.

Selected Exhibitions

2005 Wedding Belles, The Craft Centre and Design Gallery, Leeds

2004 Christmas Jewellery Exhibition, Yorkshire Sculpture Park

2004 International Jewellery London, Earls Court, London

Selected Publications

Barnes, Jo, "etcetera", Living Etc., December 2003, January and April 2004.

"August Diary", Elle Decoration, August 2003.

Hoggard, Liz, "Lookout", Crafts magazine, no. 180, January/February 2003.

Lynne Kirstin Murray

Born 1981, Glasgow, Scotland, lives and works in Edinburgh, Scotland.

Since graduating in 2003 with a first class degree from Edinburgh College of Art, Murray has exhibited throughout the UK and has been involved with teaching Drawing for Design at the college. She has recently been awarded a travel grant by The Scottish Arts Council, and was awarded The Marzee Prize in 2004.

Selected Exhibitions

2001 Schmuck, Pinakothek der Moderne, Munich

2003 New Graduate Show, Expo Arte, Oslo, Norway New Designers, Business Design Centre, London

Selected Publications

Schmuck exhibition catalogue, Pinakothek der Moderne: Munich, 2004

International Graduation Show, CITY: Gallery Marzee, 2003.

Axel Russmeyer

Born 1964, Bad Oldesloe, Germany, lives and works in Hamburg, Germany.

Axel Russmeyer obtained a diploma in Design Communication in 1993, having run his own studio in Hamburg since 1988; he has been working as a freelance designer, maker and artist since 1993. His work has been shown widely in the United States and Canada, and in London, Tokyo and around Europe. He has also produced collections for Takashimaya, Barney's, and the MoMA Design Shop in New York, as well as for Paul Smith in London.

Selected Exhibitions

2004 Chelsea Crafts Fair, London

2003 Prime Gallery, Toronto

2000 Who Knows Where or When?, Wustum Museum, Racine, WI

Selected Publications

Krautwurst, Terry, ed., 500 Beaded Objects: New Dimensions in Contemporary Beadwork, New York: Lark Books, 2004.

Hiney, Mary Jo, The Beaded Object: Making Gorgeous Flowers and Other Decorative Accents, New York: Sterling Publishing, 1997.

Acknowledgments

This book has involved many people during its research, writing and design, without whom it would not have been possible. During the research phase, Vicky Fox put together the initial list of jewellers and themes that would form the backbone of the book, followed up by indispensable work of Simone John, who brought her own knowledge of contemporary jewellery to broaden scope of the book, as well as a level of dedication, organisation and enthusiasm that made it possible to coordinate such a disparate amount of material. During the compilation of biographical information, images and text, a number of researchers and writers contributed, including Natalie Bell, Jessica Fagin, Oriana Fox, Nadia Katz-Wise, Sophie Oliver, Amy Sackville, Francis Summers, Sasha Toronyi-Lalic and Apolina Vargas. They all brought their individual approaches to jewellery, enabling order to come out of the vast amount of information that had been compiled, with the organisational expertise of Oriana and Nadia being especially welcome in the last stages.

The writers of the essays of this book, Jivan Astfalck, Caroline Broadhead and Paul Derrez — all important figures in contemporary jewellery — have given of their time and ideas with generosity and thoughtfulness, with their essays providing very different but complementary views on "new directions in jewellery". For the photo shoot that generated a number of images in this book, including the cover image, the photographer Holly Jolliffe, the models Emie Elg and Vibe Søndergaard, the especially the owners of the Straw Bale House, Sarah Wigglesworth and Jeremy Till, are all due thanks for making possible an essential component of the book's visual identity. The designer Emilia Gómez López and her assistant Hapreet Kalsi have spent many hours dealing with the huge amount of visual material included in the book to create a beautiful design that allows the variety of jewellery to maintain its individuality.

Lastly, and most importantly, thanks are due to all the jewellers who have so kindly allowed their work to be reproduced in these pages.

Catherine Grant

© 2005 Black Dog Publishing Limited,
the artists and authors
All rights reserved

Essays by Jivan Astfalck, Caroline Broadhead
and Paul Derrez

Edited by Catherine Grant

Initial research by Vicky Fox
Principal research by Simone John
Artist texts and additional research by Natalie Bell,
Jessica Fagin, Oriana Fox, Catherine Grant,
Nadia Katz-Wise, Sophie Oliver, Amy Sackville, Francis
Summers, Sasha Toronyi-Lalic and Apolina Vargas

Designed by Emilia Gómez López

Black Dog Publishing Limited
Unit 4.4 Tea Building
56 Shoreditch High Street
London
E1 6JJ

Tel: +44 (0)20 7613 1922
Fax: +44 (0)20 7613 1944
Email: info@bdp.demon.co.uk
www.bdpworld.com

All images are courtesy the jeweller or artist unless
otherwise stated

All images in Paul Derrez's essay are courtesy the
jewellers and Galerie Ra, www.galeriera.nl

Images shown on pages 39, 47, 56, 71 and 86 were
taken on location by Holly Jolliffe at the Straw Bale
House, London, courtesy of Sarah Wigglesworth and
Jeremy Till

Cover image: Kayo Saito, Floating Brooches, 2001,
polyester fibre, paper, resin, magnets and 18 ct gold,
photo: Holly Jolliffe, model: Vibe Søndergaard, shot on
location at the Straw Bale House, London, courtesy of
Sarah Wigglesworth and Jeremy Till